Contents

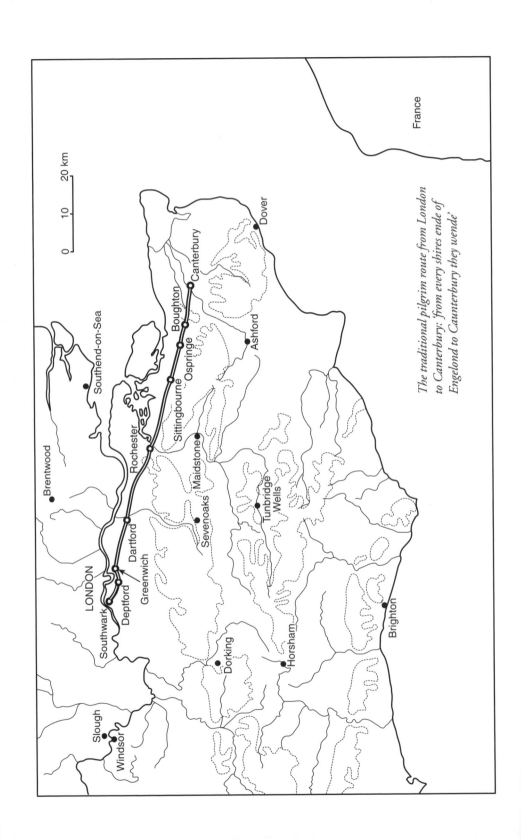

The traditional pilgrim route from London to Canterbury: 'from every shires ende of Engelond to Caunterbury they wende'

Introduction

The first encounter with a page of Chaucer in its original form can be a disconcerting experience. Initially, few words look familiar. Even when the meaning has been puzzled out, the reader is faced with an account of people who lived and died in a world very different from our own. The fourteenth century seems very far away, and you might be forgiven for thinking that *The Canterbury Tales* are too difficult.

The aim of this series is, therefore, to introduce you to the world of Chaucer in a way that will make medieval language and life as accessible as possible. With this in mind, we have adopted a layout in which each right-hand page of text is headed by a brief summary of content, and faced by a left-hand page offering a glossary of more difficult words and phrases, as well as commentary notes dealing with style, characterisation and other relevant information. There are illustrations, and suggestions for ways in which you might become involved in the text to help make it come alive.

If initial hurdles are lowered, Chaucer's wit and irony, his ability to suggest character and caricature, and his delight in raising provocative and challenging issues from various standpoints, can be more readily appreciated and enjoyed. There is something peculiarly delightful in discovering that someone who lived six hundred years ago had a sense of humour and a grasp of personalities and relationships as fresh and relevant today as it was then.

Each tale provides considerable material for fruitful discussion of fourteenth century attitudes and modern parallels. It is important to realise that the views expressed by the teller of any one tale are not necessarily Chaucer's own. Many of the activities suggested are intended to make you aware of the multiplicity of voices and attitudes in *The Canterbury Tales*. A considerable part of the enjoyment comes from awareness of the tongue-in-cheek presence of the author, who allows his characters to speak for themselves, thereby revealing their weaknesses and obsessions.

Essential information contained in each book includes a brief explanation of what *The Canterbury Tales* are, followed by some hints on handling the language. There is then a brief introduction to the teller of the relevant story, his or her portrait from the General Prologue, and an initial investigation into the techniques Chaucer uses to present characters.

The left-hand page commentaries give information applicable to the text. Finally, each book offers a full list of pilgrims, further information on Chaucer's own life and works, some background history, and greater discussion of specific medieval issues. Suggestions for essays and themes to be explored are also included. On page 112 there is a relatively short glossary of words most frequently encountered in the text, to supplement the more detailed glossary on each page.

Chaucer's tales are witty, clever and approachable, and raise interesting parallels with life today. His manipulation of the short story form is masterly. We hope this edition will bring *The Canterbury Tales* alive and allow you to appreciate Chaucer's art with ease and enjoyment.

What are The Canterbury Tales?

They are a collection of stories, loosely linked together, apparently told by a variety of storytellers with very different characters and from different social classes. In fact, both the storytellers themselves and the tales are the creation of one man, Geoffrey Chaucer. Chaucer imagines a group of pilgrims, setting off from the Tabard Inn one spring day on the long journey from London to the shrine of St Thomas Becket in Canterbury – a journey that on horseback would take about four days.

To make time pass more pleasantly they agree to tell stories to one another. Chaucer begins by introducing his pilgrims to the reader, in descriptions which do much to reveal the characters, vices and virtues of each individual. We learn more from the way each person introduces his or her tale, still more from the tales themselves and the way in which each one is told, and even further information is offered by the manner in which some pilgrims react to what others have to say. By this means Chaucer provides a witty, penetrating insight into the attitudes, weaknesses, virtues and preoccupations of English men and women of the fourteenth century. Some of their behaviour and interests may seem very strange to modern readers; at other times they seem just like us.

THE TALES

Although the complete text of *The Canterbury Tales* no longer exists, enough remains for us to appreciate the richness of texture and ironical comment Chaucer wove into his tapestry of fourteenth century life. The tales themselves are quite simple – medieval audiences did not expect original plots, but rather clever or unexpected ways of telling stories that might already be known in another form. Chaucer's audiences of educated friends, witty and urbane courtiers, perhaps the highest aristocracy and even the king and queen, were clearly able to appreciate his skills to the full. Storytelling was a leisurely process, since reading was a social rather than a private activity. Since many people could not read, Chaucer would expect the tales to be read aloud. You could try to read them like this – you will find advice on pronunciation on page 9 - and you will discover they become still more lively and dramatic when spoken rather than just read on the page.

Most of the tales in the collection include aspects of at least one of the following categories of tales familiar to Chaucer's audience.

Courtly romances These courtly love affairs were for the upper classes. They often told of unrequited love from a distance, the male lover suffering sleepless nights of anguish, pining away, writing poetry, serenading his beloved with love songs and performing brave feats of noble daring. Meanwhile the beloved (but untouchable) lady would sit in her bower and sew, walk in her castle gardens, set her lover impossible tasks to accomplish, and give him a scarf or handkerchief as a keepsake. Chaucer enjoys poking gentle fun at the rarefied atmosphere of such stories.

Fabliaux Extended jokes or tricks, often bawdy, and usually full of sexual innuendo.

The destination of the pilgrims – Canterbury Cathedral today

Fables These are tales that make a moral point, often using animals as characters.

Sermons Sermons were stories with a moral message. Since 95 per cent of society could not read, sermons had to be good, interesting and full of dramatic storytelling. The line between a good story and a good sermon was very thin indeed. Usually there was an abstract theme (gluttony, avarice, pride) and much use was made of biblical and classical parallels or *exempla* to underline the preacher's point.

Confessions The storytellers often look back over their own lives, revealing faults and unhappinesses to the audience. This aspect is usually introduced in the teller's prologue to the actual story.

The tales vary widely in content and tone, since medieval stories, Chaucer's included, were supposed both to instruct and to entertain. Many, like the Nun's Priest's Tale, have an underlying moral; some, such as the Pardoner's Tale, are highly dramatic, and others, like those told by the Knight and the Squire, have their origins firmly in the courtly love tradition. But many are more complex than this suggests. They also vary greatly: Chaucer includes stories as sentimental as that of the Prioress, and as crude and bawdy as those of the Miller and the Reeve.

   The device of using different characters to tell different tales allows Chaucer to distance himself from what is being said, and to disguise the fact that he controls the varied and opinionated voices of his creations. He can pretend, for instance, to have no way of preventing the drunken Miller from telling his vulgar story about the carpenter's wife, and he can absolve himself from blame when the tellers become sexually explicit. A modern audience may find his frankness and openness about sex surprising, but it was understandable, for there was little privacy, even for the well-to-do, and sexual matters were no secret. The coarse satire of the fabliaux was as much enjoyed by Chaucer's 'gentil' audience as the more restrained romances.

7

Chaucer's language

The unfamiliar appearance of a page of Chaucerian English often prevents students from pursuing their investigations any further. It does no good telling them that this man used language with a complexity and subtlety not found in any writer of English anywhere before him. They remain unimpressed. He looks incomprehensible.

In fact, with a little help, it does not take very long to master Chaucer's language. Much of the vocabulary is the same, or at least very similar to, words we use today. On page 112 there is a glossary of the unfamiliar words most frequently used in this text, and these will quickly become familiar. Other words and phrases that could cause difficulties are explained on the pages facing the actual text.

The language of Chaucer is known as Middle English – a term which covers the English language as it was written and spoken in the period roughly between 1150 and 1500. It is difficult to be more precise than this, for Middle English itself was changing and developing throughout that period towards 'modern' English.

Old English (Anglo-Saxon) was spoken and written until around 1066, the time of the Norman Conquest. This event put power and authority in England into the hands of the Norman lords, who spoke their own brand of Norman French. Inevitably this became the language of the upper classes. The effect was felt in the church, for speedily the control of the monasteries and nunneries was given to members of the new French-speaking aristocracy. Since these religious houses were the seats of learning and centres of literacy, the effect on language was considerable. If you were a wealthy Anglo-Saxon, eager to get on in the world of your new over-lords, you learnt French. Many people were bi- or even trilingual. French was the language of the law courts and much international commerce; Latin was the language of learning (from elementary school to the highest levels of scholarship) and of the church (from parish church services to the great international institution of the papacy).

Gradually, as inter-marriages between Norman French and English families became more common, the distinction between the two groups and the two languages became blurred. Many French words became absorbed into Old English, making it more like the language we speak today. In the thirteenth century King John lost control of his Norman lands, and as hostility between England and France grew, a sense of English nationalism strengthened. In 1362 the English language was used for the first time in an English parliament. At the same time, Geoffrey Chaucer, a young ex-prisoner of war, was sharpening his pens and his wit, testing the potential for amusement, satire and beauty in this rich, infinitely variable, complex literary tool.

Although some tales are partly, or entirely, in prose, *The Canterbury Tales* are written largely in rhyming iambic couplets. This form of regular metre and rhyme is flexible enough to allow Chaucer to write in a range of styles. He uses the couplet form to imitate colloquial speech as easily as philosophical debate. Most importantly, Chaucer wrote poetry 'for the ear'; it is written for the listener, as much as for the reader. Rhyme and alliteration add emphasis and link ideas and objects together in a way that is satisfying for the audience. The words jog along as easily and comfortably as the imaginary pilgrims and their horses jogged to Canterbury.

PRONUNCIATION

Chaucer spoke the language of London, of the king's court, but he was well aware of differences in dialect and vocabulary in other parts of the country. In the Reeve's Tale, for instance, he mocks the north-country accents of the two students. It is clear, therefore, that there were differences in pronunciation in the fourteenth century, just as there are today.

Having been told that Chaucer wrote verse to be read aloud, students may be dismayed to find that they do not know how it should sound. There are two encouraging things to bear in mind. The first is that although scholars feel fairly sure they know something about how Middle English sounded, they cannot be certain, and a number of different readings can still be heard. The second concerns the strong metrical and rhyming structure Chaucer employed in the writing of his tales.

Finding the rhythm Follow the rhythm of the verse (iambic pentameter), sounding or omitting the final 'e' syllable in the word as seems most appropriate. In the line
> **Unto the herte, ne koude in no manere**
it would add an unnecessary syllable if the final 'e' in 'herte' and 'koude' were to be pronounced. An 'e' at the end of a word almost always disappears if it is followed by a word beginning with a vowel or 'h'.

In the case of these examples:
> **Then herke why, I sey nat this for noght,**
and
> **And somme were riche, and hadden badde name**
the best swing to the regular ten-syllabled line is achieved by sounding the 'e' (as a neutral vowel sound, like the 'u' in put, or the 'a' in about) in the words 'herke' and 'badde', but not in 'somme' or 'riche'.

Other points In words beginning with the letter 'y' (for example 'ywet', 'yknowe') the 'y' is sounded as it would be in the modern 'party'. Many consonants now silent were pronounced – as in 'knight', 'wrong'. All the consonants would be given voice in words such as 'draughtes' and 'knight' and the 'gh' would be sounded like the Scots 'ch' in 'loch'. The combination 'ow' (for example 'yow', meaning 'you') is pronounced as 'how', and the 'ei' in 'streit' would be like the 'a' sound in 'pay'.

For more ideas of what the language might have sounded like, listen to the recordings of Chaucer published by Cambridge University Press and by the 'Chaucer Man' (Trevor Eaton).

WARM-UP ACTIVITIES

• In groups of three using the Merchant's Prologue, one person read the narrator, one the Merchant and the other the Host, trying to get a sense of the feelings of the speakers.
• Choose a long, self-contained section from the text: lines 125-149 of the

Merchant's Tale are a useful example. After a brief explanation of the content, if considered necessary, students should work in pairs, speaking alternately, and changing over at each punctuation point. It should be possible to develop a fair turn of speed without losing the sense of the passage.

• Again in pairs, choose about ten lines of text; as one of the pair maintains a steady beat [^/^/^/^/^/] the partner does his or her best to fit the words to the rhythm.

• Choose a long self-contained unit from the text, such as one of Placebo's speeches or the description of the marriage feast. Students should walk round the room, speaking the script, and turning left or right at each punctuation mark.

GRAMMATICAL POINTS

Emphatic negatives Whereas a person who stated that 'he wasn't going nowhere, not never' might be considered grammatically incorrect nowadays, Chaucer used double or triple negatives quite often, to give a statement powerful added emphasis. One of the best known is in his description of the Knight in the General Prologue:

> He never yet no vilenye sayde
> In al his life, unto no manner wight.

Another occurs in the Merchant's Tale:

> That ther nis no so greet felicitee
> In mariage, ne nevere mo shal bee,

In both cases the repeated negative strengthens the force of what is being said.

Word elision In modern written English words and phrases are often run together (elided) to represent the spoken form of these words – 'didn't', 'can't', 'won't', 'I've', and so on. Chaucer uses short forms of words too, especially in forming the negative. In his time it was usual to form a negative by placing 'ne' before the verb. With common verbs this was often elided into the verb. Thus 'ne was' is the Chaucerian form of 'was not', but it was often written as 'nas'.

The 'y' prefix The past tense of a verb sometimes has a 'y' before the rest of the verb, particularly in past participles:

That blosmeth er that fruit ywoxen be	That blossoms before the fruit is grown
Whan that he was in his bed ybrought	When his servants had brought him to bed

The 'possessive' form of nouns In modern English we indicate possession by means of an apostrophe: 'the hat of the man' becomes 'the man's hat'. Middle English had a particular formation that is still used in modern German. Where we now use an apostrophe followed by an 's', Chaucer uses the suffix 'es'. So 'the man's hat' becomes 'the mannes hat', the extra 'n' indicating that the word has two syllables.

The Merchant's contribution

Chaucer promises at the beginning of *The Canterbury Tales* that he will describe all his pilgrims, telling the audience something of their status and their personality. He lists them in rough order of precedence, beginning with the Knight and his party (his son, the Squire, and their Yeoman servant). He continues with the group of religious characters who have status and importance (the Prioress, the Monk and the Friar), and then moves down through the social ranks, listing well-to-do middle class individuals and those with some wealth, followed by more lowly commoners. He ends his lists with two unashamedly corrupt servants of the church, the Summoner and the Pardoner. This introduction has come to be known as the 'General Prologue'. A list of the pilgrims who feature in the complete work may be found on page 100.

In the General Prologue, the Merchant is described as secretive and devious. He is not given a name. Many of the pilgrims are not named but in this case Chaucer draws attention to the fact by telling us that he does not know the Merchant's name, adding to the impression of secrecy. As well as being a merchant he is probably a moneylender, and he boasts about his profits. We are also told that he is in debt, but that no one could have guessed from his manner. Chaucer calls him 'worthy' or honourable twice, and this is what the Merchant calls January in the second line of his tale. As it soon becomes clear that January is not at all 'worthy', this casts doubts on the Merchant's own worthiness.

The Merchant bursts into his Prologue without any invitation by the Host. His first lines are apparently in bitter response to the final words of the Clerk who has just told the tale of Patient Griselda. This story of an unnaturally patient and faithful wife comes some time after the tale of the Wife of Bath. Her Prologue and Tale have been about women getting the better of men in marriage. Both the Clerk and the Merchant refer to the Wife of Bath, bringing to life the social group of pilgrims as they discuss each other's stories. The Merchant's misery in his marriage seems intense, and though he specifically says that he cannot talk any more about himself and his own marriage, there is a strong sense of personal involvement between the Merchant, as narrator of the Tale, and January, the knight of the Tale.

The Merchant's Tale is unusual in *The Canterbury Tales*. Many of the tales deal with corruption, or are told by corrupt narrators, but there is often a degree of irony and humour which prevents the story from being too unpleasant. Chaucer seems deliberately to expose January to the reader as thoroughly disagreeable, and his marriage to the young woman, May, as obscene. May and her lover, Damyan, do not escape condemnation; they are equally depraved.

Chaucer's description of the Merchant's clothes, and his interest in the trade with Middleberg suggests that he is intended to be seen as a wool merchant.

- Chaucer's description of the Merchant does not mention religion. Why might he be on a pilgrimage?
- Write a detailed description of a similar kind of person from the twenty-first century, who might be making a journey. You could try re-drafting your description into iambic pentameter.
- What kind of person is the Merchant? With a partner pick out all the details that Chaucer gives the reader and, like a detective, see what you can deduce.

272   **forked berd** [This was a very fashionable kind of beard.]

273   **mottelee** parti-coloured cloth [a fashionable fabric]

        hye on horse on a high saddle

274   **Flaundrissh bever hat** an elegant hat from Flanders [This suggests that he either trades with, or has visited the continent.]

275   **His bootes clasped faire and fetisly** his boots had a neat and elegant fastening

276-7   **His resons ... th'encrees of his winning** he gave his opinions very solemnly, and was always concerned with the increase of his profits

278-9   **He wolde the see ... Orwelle** he wanted the sea trade between Middleberg (in Holland) and

Orwell (on the English coast) to be protected at all costs

280   **Wel koude he in eschaunge sheeldes selle** [A 'sheelde' was a unit of exchange. Selling 'sheeldes' was a way of borrowing money but often at the expense of the seller.]

281   **ful wel his wit bisette** he used his wits well

282-4   **Ther wiste no wight ... chevissaunce** he was so dignified in his behaviour concerning his bargains and his financial arrangements that no-one knew that he was in debt

285   **with alle** indeed

286   **I noot how men him calle** I do not know his name

The description of the Merchant in the General Prologue.

A Marchant was ther with a forked berd,
In mottelee, and hye on horse he sat;
Upon his heed a Flaundrissh bever hat,
His bootes clasped faire and fetisly.   275
His resons he spak ful solempnely,
Sowninge alwey th'encrees of his winning.
He wolde the see were kept for any thing
Bitwixe Middelburgh and Orewelle.
Wel koude he in eschaunge sheeldes selle.   280
This worthy man ful wel his wit bisette:
Ther wiste no wight that he was in dette,
So estatly was he of his governaunce
With his bargaines and with his chevissaunce.
For sothe he was a worthy man with alle,   285
But, sooth to seyn, I noot how men him calle.

The Merchant as depicted in the Ellesmere manuscript. This was written and decorated in the fifteenth century but reproduced the styles of dress of the 1380s

13

The first line of the Merchant's Prologue is an echo of the last line of Chaucer's epilogue to the Clerk's Tale which concludes the Clerk's final comments: 'And let him care, and wepe and wringe and waille'. Although the manuscript of *The Canterbury Tales* is fragmentary, scholars agree that the Clerk's Tale was intended immediately to precede the Merchant's Prologue and Tale. The Clerk tells a tale which also concerns the marriage of a knight, Walter, who lived in Lombardy. He is persuaded by his people that he should marry and he chooses a virtuous but extremely poor bride, Griselda. Before they marry he makes her promise to obey him in thought, word and deed. He tests her promise beyond all reason. The Clerk tells the other pilgrims that his story is not about mortal women but is an image of the ideal relationship between Christ and his church. For more information on the Clerk's Tale see page 108.

- Sometimes it is more effective to leave the reader to imagine the precise details of your story as the Merchant does here. Discuss with a partner what you think the Merchant's wife might have done to upset him so much in such a short time. Compare your ideas with those of another pair. (Some of you may wish to revise your thoughts when you have read the whole tale.)

2	**even and a-morwe** night and day
	other mo many more
7-8	**For thogh ... him overmacche** even if she were married to the devil she would defeat him
9-10	**What sholde ... shrewe at al** Why should I tell you of her cruelty in detail? She is a complete shrew
12	**Grisildis** [the unnaturally patient wife of the Clerk's Tale]
13	**passing** extreme
14	**also moot I thee** as I hope to prosper
15	**I wolde ... in the snare** I would never again enter the trap [marriage]
17	**Assaye whoso wole** try it who will
18	**Seint Thomas of Inde** Doubting Thomas [One of Christ's disciples who would not believe in the resurrection of Christ until he had put his hands in the wounds. He is supposed to have performed his ministry in India.]
19-20	**As for the moore ... so bifalle!** For the majority of men, I don't say all, God forbid it should be true
21	**goode sire Hoost** Good sir Host [the Host of the Tabard Inn in Southwark who was accompanying the pilgrims to Canterbury]
22	**Thise monthes ... pardee** no longer than two months, by God
24-25	**rive Unto the herte** split him to the heart
31-32	**but of ... may namoore** but of my own pain, for my suffering heart, I cannot speak more

In his prologue the Merchant tells his audience about his own adversity in his short married life.
He has suffered so much that he feels unable to go into any details. The Host encourages him to tell
a story about marriage since he is so experienced. The Merchant agrees but refuses to speak any
more about his own life.

'Weping and wailing, care and oother sorwe
I knowe ynogh, on even and a-morwe,'
Quod the Marchant, 'and so doon other mo
That wedded been. I trowe that it be so,
For wel I woot it fareth so with me. 5
I have a wyf, the worste that may be;
For thogh the feend to hire ycoupled were,
She wolde him overmacche, I dar wel swere.
What sholde I yow reherce in special
Hir hye malice? She is a shrewe at al. 10
Ther is a long and large difference
Bitwix Grisildis grete pacience
And of my wyf the passing crueltee.
Were I unbounden, also moot I thee,
I wolde nevere eft comen in the snare. 15
We wedded men liven in sorwe and care.
Assaye whoso wole, and he shal finde
That I seye sooth, by Seint Thomas of Inde,
As for the moore part, I sey nat alle.
God shilde that it sholde so bifalle! 20
    A, goode sire Hoost, I have ywedded bee
Thise monthes two, and moore nat, pardee;
And yet, I trowe, he that al his live
Wyflees hath been, though that men wolde him rive
Unto the herte, ne koude in no manere 25
Tellen so muchel sorwe as I now heere
Koude tellen of my wyves cursednesse!'
    'Now,' quod oure Hoost, 'Marchaunt, so God yow blesse,
Sin ye so muchel knowen of that art
Ful hertely I pray yow telle us part.' 30
    'Gladly,' quod he, 'but of myn owene soore,
For soory herte, I telle may namoore.'

Paradise (or the Garden of Eden), is an image that runs through the Merchant's Tale. It is a reference to Genesis chapter 3 where God creates the Garden of Eden for Adam and Eve, and where they live in perfect happiness until Eve is tempted by the serpent to eat the fruit of the forbidden tree; the tree of the knowledge of good and evil. In punishment God ejects Adam and Eve from the garden. In literature any reference to Paradise or to the Garden of Eden carries with it the implicit threat of the serpent and a consequent fall from grace.

- The Merchant calls the knight 'worthy' or honourable. As you read on, consider whether this knight is truly an honourable man. The Merchant also leaves the reader to decide whether the knight decides to marry out of holiness, or the foolishness of extreme old age. What do you think?
- Read aloud lines 33–50, first to get the general meaning and then to understand the tone and rhythm. Work out how to do it after reading the section on Chaucer's language on page 8.
- What is the effect of the narrator's statement 'I kan nat seye' in line 42?
- In line 58 the Merchant calls a wife 'the fruit of his tresor'. As you read on bear this conflict of images in mind.

33	**Whilom** once	58	**fruit of his tresor** *literally:* fruit of his treasure [The Merchant combines two images; that of life, 'fruit', and money, 'treasure'.]
36	**a wyflees man** a single (wifeless) man		
37	**folwed ay ... his appetit** he always obeyed his sexual desire for women	59	**feir** beautiful
38	**seculeer** not in holy orders [and therefore not vowed to chastity]	60	**On which ... heir** on whom he might father an heir
41	**Were it for hoolinesse or for dotage** either because of piety or senility		
42	**I kan nat seye** I cannot tell		
	corage desire		
49-50	**boond, bond** the bond of marriage [but it also reminds us of the Merchant's own desire to be 'unbounden' line 14]		
51	**worth a bene** [Not being worth 'a bean' suggests the worthlessness of any state than matrimony.]		
52	**clene** wholesome		
53	**paradis** Paradise – the Garden of Eden		
57	**hoor** white-haired		

Medieval merchants

The Merchant sets his tale in Pavia, a city in Lombardy, famous at the time for bankers and brothels. It concerns an elderly wealthy knight, who, having been single all his life, decides to marry. Though he has never hesitated to satisfy his sexual appetite, he now considers matrimony the perfect state and he also wants an heir.

    Whilom ther was dwellinge in Lumbardye
A worthy knight, that born was of Pavie,
In which he lived in greet prosperitee;   35
And sixty yeer a wyflees man was hee,
And folwed ay his bodily delit
On wommen, ther as was his appetit,
As doon thise fooles that been seculeer.
And whan that he was passed sixty yeer,   40
Were it for hoolinesse or for dotage,
I kan nat seye, but swich a greet corage
Hadde this knight to been a wedded man
That day and night he dooth al that he kan
T'espien where he mighte wedded be,   45
Preyinge oure Lord to graunten him that he
Mighte ones knowe of thilke blisful lyf
That is bitwixe an housbonde and his wyf,
And for to live under that hooly boond
With which that first God man and womman bond. 50
'Noon oother lyf,' seyde he, 'is worth a bene;
For wedlok is so esy and so clene,
That in this world it is a paradis.'
Thus seyde this olde knight, that was so wis.
    And certeinly, as sooth as God is king,   55
To take a wif it is a glorious thing,
And namely whan a man is oold and hoor;
Thanne is a wyf the fruit of his tresor.
Thanne sholde he take a yong wif and a feir,
On which he mighte engendren him an heir,   60
And lede his lyf in joye and in solas,
Where as thise bacheleris singe 'allas,'
Whan that they finden any adversitee
In love, which nis but childissh vanitee.

- What are your initial thoughts on the Merchant's defence of marriage? Make some detailed notes on his ideas about the benefits of having a wife, and add to them as your ideas develop in later pages.
- Consider what the Merchant might be suggesting in lines 86-92 about the relationship between master and manservant. You might like to come back to this point when you have finished the Tale.

67-8	**On brotel ... sikernesse** they build on sandy and unstable ground when they expect to find security
69-70	**They live ... noon arreest** they live like birds or beasts, in freedom and under no restraint
71-3	**Ther as ... ybounde** whereas in the bonds of matrimony the married man lives a happy and ordered life [However, a yoke can also bind unwilling partners.]
75	**buxom** obedient
76-7	**eek so ententif ... make?** also so attentive to care for him in sickness and in health as a wife? [In the traditional Christian marriage service the wife promises to care for her husband in sickness and in health, whether he is rich or poor.]
78	**For wele ... forsake** she will not forsake him for happiness or sorrow
79	**nis nat wery** will never weary of [note the double negative for emphasis]
80	**bedrede** bedridden
	sterve dies
83	**What force ... lye?** what does it matter if Theophrastus wants to lie? [Theophrastus (c.372-287 BC) was the author of the satiric *Golden Book of Marriage*.]
84	**housbondrye** household economy
85	**dispence** expenditure
86	**dooth moore diligence** works harder
87	**good** goods, property
90	**verray freendes** true friends
	trewe knave faithful servant
91-2	**she that waiteth ay After thy good** she who has been waiting for ages to inherit your property
94	**cokewold** cuckold [a man whose wife is unfaithful, usually presented in literature and art as a figure of fun]

The Merchant speaks of the potential joys and comforts of marriage. He rejects the writings of experts such as Theophrastus who warn that wives can bring distress, that servants or friends can care more for a man and his property, and that a wife can be unfaithful.

And trewely it sit wel to be so,   65
That bacheleris have often peyne and wo;
On brotel ground they builde, and brotelnesse
They find, whan they wene sikernesse.
They live but as a brid or as a beest,
In libertee, and under noon arreest;   70
Ther as a wedded man in his estaat
Liveth a lyf blisful and ordinaat,
Under this yok of mariage ybounde.
Wel may his herte in joy and blisse habounde,
For who kan be so buxom as a wyf?   75
Who is so trewe, and eek so entenif
To kepe him, sik and hool, as is his make?
For wele or wo she wole him nat forsake;
She nis nat wery him to love and serve,
Thogh that he lye bedrede, til he sterve.   80
And yet somme clerkes seyn it nis nat so,
Of whiche he Theofraste is oon of tho.
What force though Theofraste liste lye?
'Ne take no wyf,' quod he, 'for housbondrye,
As for to spare in houshold thy dispence.   85
A trewe servant dooth moore diligence
Thy good to kepe, than thyn owene wyf,
For she wol claime half part al hir lyf.
And if that thou be sik, so God me save,
Thy verray freendes, or a trewe knave,   90
Wol kepe thee bet than she that waiteth ay
After thy good and hath doon many a day.
And if thou take a wyf unto thyn hoold,
Ful lightly mystow been a cokewold.'

In lines 99-103 the Merchant equates God's gift of a wife with material goods. The detailed list shows how important property is to him. He is deluding himself if he assumes that the acquisition of a wife can be regarded in the same way as the purchase of a field or a table. What, or who, is missing from his calculations?

Although the Merchant sees the creation of Eve, helpmeet and companion to Adam, as evidence of God's goodness, consider the outcome of this story from Genesis and the implications it might have for the knight's marriage. Chaucer's audience would be well aware that Eve tempted Adam into sin and caused the downfall of mankind.

• Bearing in mind that the Merchant is talking about the Garden of Eden when he talks about God's creation of Eve, how do you feel that his audience might react to the exaggerated language in lines 119-24? Read these lines aloud and think about the effect Chaucer is creating with word order and the rhyme.

95	**sentence** opinion	108	**shent** damned or ruined
96	**ther God his bones corse** God curse his bones	110	**I speke … estaat** I speak of those not in holy orders
97	**But take … herke me** but take no heed of all this illusion, defy Theophrastus and listen to me	112	**ywroght** made
		113	**hie** high
		118	**heerby may ye preve** thus you may prove
100-3	**Alle … upon a wal** all other kinds of gift, certainly, such as land, income, pasture or common land, or furnishings, are all gifts from Fortune, and will pass like a shadow on a wall [This detailed list of property is revealing as it shows where the Merchant's values lie.]	120	**His paradis … disport** his earthly paradise and his pleasure
		121-2	**So buxom … in unitee** because she is so obedient and virtuous they are bound to live in harmony [You might like to consider the irony of this as you read on.]
104-6	**But drede … paraventure** but doubt not, if I speak plainly, a wife will last and remain in your house even longer than you wish, perhaps	123-4	**O flessh … distresse** they are one flesh – and one flesh, I believe, has one heart in happiness and in sorrow
107	**sacrement** [Marriage is one of the major sacraments of the church.]		

The Merchant continues to speak of the benefits of having a wife. He justifies the desire to marry by referring to a wife as God's gift to a man.

This sentence, and an hundred thinges worse,   95
Writeth this man, ther God his bones corse!
But take no kep of al swich vanitee;
Deffie Theofraste, and herke me.
   A wyf is Goddes yifte verraily;
Alle othere manere yiftes hardily,   100
As londes, rentes, pasture, or commune,
Or moebles, alle been yiftes of Fortune,
That passen as a shadwe upon a wal.
But drede nat, if pleynly speke I shal,
A wif wol laste, and in thyn hous endure,   105
Wel lenger than thee list, paraventure.
   Mariage is a ful greet sacrement.
He which that hath no wyf, I holde him shent;
He liveth helplees and al desolat,—
I speke of folk in seculer estaat.   110
And herke why, I sey nat this for noght,
That womman is for mannes helpe ywroght.
The hie God, whan he hadde Adam maked,
And saugh him al allone, bely-naked;
God of his grete goodnesse seyde than,   115
'Lat us now make an helpe unto this man
Lyk to himself'; and thanne He made him Eve.
Heere may ye se, and heerby may ye preve,
That wyf is mannes helpe and his confort;
His paradis terrestre, and his disport.   120
So buxom and so vertuous is she,
They moste nedes live in unitee.
O flessh they ben, and o fleesh, as I gesse,
Hath but oon herte, in wele and in distresse.

- Do you think that the Merchant is really talking about a wife when he speaks of this obedient companion? Make a list of the things that you consider important about a partner in marriage. Would some men still secretly like a wife who was entirely subservient, who did everything that her husband wanted and never contradicted him?
- Improvise two scenes, one an episode in the life of the 'perfect wife' (and fortunate husband) followed by a more realistic presentation.
- Write a private diary entry by the 'perfect wife' giving her side of the story.
- From the point of view of a woman looking for a 'perfect husband', write an account of what you would be looking for.

125   **A wyf ... *benedicite*** a wife, bless us, Saint Mary! [an exclamation]

128   **tweye** two

130   **swinke** work

131   **never a deel** absolutely nothing

132   **Al that ... weel** everything that pleases her husband, pleases her

133   **ones** once

135-6   **O blisful ... vertuous** O wedlock, you are so merry and so moral [This is a rhetorical device called an apostrophe where the narrator addresses an object. The tone is that of a sermon.]

138-40   **every ... wyf** every self-respecting man should thank God on his knees for sending him a wife

143   **sikernesse** security

145   **So that he werke after his wyves reed** if he follows his wife's advice

147-9   **They been ... rede** they are so faithful and full of wisdom that if you want to be wise, always follow a woman's advice

'Do this,' he seith; 'Al redy, sire' seith she

22

The Merchant continues to extol the conveniences of marriage from a man's point of view. He says a wife will be always helpful and obedient.

A wyf, a, Seinte Marie, *benedicite*,   125
How mighte a man han any adversitee
That hath a wyf? Certes, I kan nat seye.
The blisse which that is bitwixe hem tweye
Ther may no tonge telle, or herte thinke.
If he be povre, she helpeth him to swinke;   130
She kepeth his good, and wasteth never a deel;
Al that hire housbonde lust, hire liketh weel;
She seith nat ones 'nay', whan he seith 'ye.'
'Do this,' seith he; 'Al redy, sire,' seith she.
O blisful ordre of wedlok precious,   135
Thou art so murye, and eek so vertuous,
And so commended and appreved eek
That every man that halt him worth a leek,
Upon his bare knees oughte al his lyf
Thanken his God that him hath sent a wyf,   140
Or elles preye to God him for to sende
A wyf, to laste unto his lives ende.
For thanne his lyf is set in sikernesse;
He may nat be deceyved, as I gesse,
So that he werke after his wyves reed.   145
Thanne may he boldely beren up his heed,
They been so trewe, and therwithal so wise;
For which, if thou wolt werken as the wise,
Do alwey so as wommen wol thee rede.

In lines 150-62, though the Merchant chooses examples of women who are resourceful and successful, they also have the theme of deception in common. The story of Jacob and Rebecca is told in Genesis chapter 27. He was her younger son and she wanted him to inherit his father's wealth, so she made Isaac, his elderly blind father, believe that he was Esau, his brother, by tying a goat-skin over him. Judith's story is told in chapters 12 and 13 of the book of Judith in the Apocrypha. She saved the Israelites by going to the camp of the enemy Assyrians, seducing their hero, Holofernes, and then beheading him when he was asleep and drunk. From I Samuel chapter 25 comes the story of Abigail. She was the wife of Nabal and she pleaded with King David not to punish her husband. David was so charmed by her that he married her after the death of Nabal. In the book of Esther chapter 7, Esther saves her people by persuading the King to hang Haman on the gallows that he had prepared for Mordechai.

• Discuss the potential irony here. Chaucer is creating a narrator who does not see that his list of 'virtuous' women might be viewed quite differently by his audience.
• In groups, choose one of the stories and re-enact it for the rest of the class. Would you choose to emphasise the trickery – or the resourcefulness?

152	**Boond** bound
153	**benison** blessing
155	**conseil** advice, counsel
156	**slow** killed, slew
162	**him Mardochee Of Assuere enhaunced for to be** arranged for Mordechai (Mardochee) to be promoted by her husband Ahasuerus (Assuere)
163-4	**Ther nis ... wyf** as Seneca says, there is nothing better than a humble wife [Seneca was a stoic philosopher and playwright. His life was known for its austerity.]
165	**Suffre ... bit** endure your wife's commands as Cato tells you
169	**Wel may ... kepe** a sick man may well weep and wail because there is no wife to look after his house [This may well strike the reader as ironic, when the Merchant has begun his Prologue talking about his own weeping and wailing caused by his wife.]

171	**if wisely thou wolt wirche** if you wish to act wisely
172	**Love wel ... chirche** love your wife as Christ loves his church [This is a reference to the traditional Christian marriage service where the congregation is reminded that the relationship between the man and the woman in marriage was designed to be a reflection of the relationship between Christ and his church. The Clerk has referred to this in his Tale.]
173-5	**If thou ... thee** [This is from a well-known passage in Paul's letter to the Ephesians: man and wife are one flesh, therefore you should love your wife as you love yourself.]
175	**fostreth** cares for
177	**jape or pleye** joke or tease
178	**holden the siker weye** keep the safe path
179	**knit** united
180	**namely** especially

To give authority to his views on marriage, the Merchant gives examples from the Old Testament and from ancient philosophers.

Lo, how that Jacob, as thise clerkes rede,   150
By good conseil of his mooder Rebekke,
Boond the kides skin aboute his nekke,
For which his fadres benison he wan.
  Lo Judith, as the storie eek telle kan,
By wis conseil she Goddes peple kepte,   155
And slow him Olofernus, whil he slepte.
  Lo Abigail, by good conseil, how she
Saved hir housbonde Nabal, whan that he
Sholde han be slain; and looke, Ester also
By good conseil delivered out of wo   160
The peple of God, and made him Mardochee
Of Assuere enhaunced for to be.
  Ther nis no thing in gree superlatif,
As seith Senek, above an humble wyf.
  Suffre thy wives tonge, as Catoun bit;   165
She shal comande, and thou shalt suffren it,
And yet she wole obeye of curteisye.
A wif is kepere of thyn housbondrye;
Wel may the sike man biwaille and wepe,
Ther as ther nis no wyf the hous to kepe.   170
I warne thee, if wisely thou wolt wirche,
Love wel thy wyf, as Crist loved his chirche.
If thou lovest thyself, thou lovest thy wyf;
No man hateth his flessh, but in his lyf
He fostreth it, and therfore bidde I thee,   175
Cherisse thy wyf, or thou shalt nevere thee.
Housbonde and wyf, what so men jape or pleye,
Of worldly folk holden the siker weye;
They been so knit ther may noon harm bitide,
And namely upon the wyves side.   180

If January really thinks he is dying: 'on my pittes brinke', perhaps he should be thinking of his soul like St Jerome, not about how much younger than him his wife should be. St Jerome (c.347-419) was an ascetic who translated the Bible into Latin.

- Lines 181-4 are a narrative comment by the narrator, the Merchant. What might he be thinking here? In pairs, one person should speak the narrator's lines twice as persuasively and convincingly as you can, first to set the meaning, and then to include the tone and rhythm. The second person should say what they feel might be in the Merchant's mind as he tells this part of his story.
- What do you think of January's use of animal imagery in lines 206-8? Read aloud lines 203-210 trying various tones – lecherous, aggressive, arrogant, complacent. Share your ideas with others in your group and listen to their suggestions. Which seems to you to be more appropriate to the character of January?
- Once he has made the decision to marry, January loses no time, and he asks his friends to look out for a suitable 'mayde fair and tendre of age'. Debates on the benefits or otherwise of marriage were a popular kind of male writing in the Middle Ages. Do you think it is a good idea to ask friends to find you a suitable marriage partner?
- Between lines 193 and 199 find words which suggest January's haste. He has no affection for any specific woman, just one who fits his specifications.

182	**inwith his dayes olde** in his old age	205	**She ... certain** she certainly won't be older than twenty [In some manuscripts this reads 'sixteen'.]
183	**lusty** pleasant		
187	**sad** serious	206	**Oold fissh ... fain** I prefer mature fish and young meat [Chaucer's use of animal imagery in lines 206-8 is significant: a pike and a bull are aggressive creatures. This hardly reflects the honey-sweet quiet of lines 183-4 and the image of 'yong flessh' gives a disturbing insight into his fantasies. There also seems a wilful self-deception as he is old himself.]
188	**hoor** white-haired		
189	**pittes brinke** on the edge of my grave (pit)		
191	**I have ... despended** I have foolishly wasted my life [He uses the word 'despended' which could refer to a financial transaction. Do you think the Merchant is being ironic, or the poet?]		
196	**shapeth** prepare		
198	**fonde t'espien** try to find	210	**It is ... forage** It is only dried bean-stalks and coarse fodder [i.e. rough and unproductive – January's coarseness here prepares the reader for the contrast between his idealising of the married state and the reality of his actions.]
200-2	**But ... allyen** because there are more of you, you will be able to spot more quickly a likely girl for me to marry		
204	**I wol ... manere** there is no way that I will have an old wife [Chaucer's use of the double negative here gives emphasis to January's determination.]		

January, the central character of the tale, calls his friends to him in order to tell them that he has decided that, because he is getting old, it is time for him to marry. He will only marry a girl who is less than twenty years old.

For which this Januarie, of whom I tolde,
Considered hath, inwith his dayes olde,
The lusty lyf, the vertuous quiete,
That is in mariage hony-sweete;
And for his freendes on a day he sente,   185
To tellen hem th'effect of his entente.
   With face sad his tale he hath hem toold.
He sayde, 'Freendes, I am hoor and oold,
And almoost, God woot, on my pittes brinke;
Upon my soule somwhat moste I thinke.   190
I have my body folily despended;
Blessed be God that it shal been amended.
For I wol be, certeyn, a wedded man,
And that anoon in al the haste I kan.
Unto som mayde fair and tendre of age,   195
I prey yow, shapeth for my mariage
Al sodeynly, for I wol nat abide;
And I wol fonde t'espien, on my side,
To whom I may be wedded hastily.
But forasmuche as ye been mo than I,   200
Ye shullen rather swich a thing espyen
Than I, and where me best were to allyen.
   But o thing warne I yow, my freendes deere,
I wol noon oold wyf han in no manere.
She shal nat passe twenty yeer, certain;   205
Oold fissh and yong flessh wolde I have ful fain.
Bet is,' quod he, 'a pyk than a pikerel,
And bet than old boef is the tendre veel.
I wol no womman thritty yeer of age;
It is but bene-straw and greet forage.   210

Chaucer gives a sense of verisimilitude to the whole of *The Canterbury Tales* by occasional references to other tales or tellers. Here the mention of 'thise olde widwes' who are so crafty and skilful at disturbing their husband's peace seems to be a direct reference to the Wife of Bath.

January uses the image of 'warm wax' when he thinks of a malleable young girl. The image of wax is returned to later in the Tale.

- Having claimed that he wants to marry to enjoy a quiet and virtuous life for the benefit of his soul, January now adds a further reason in lines 227-8. How does Chaucer's use of imagery here suggest that this is an important consideration for January?

- In small groups, compare January's reasons for refusing to marry an old woman. Look particularly at lines 220-8. What impression have you gained of the knight so far? Make a summary of the points which seem to you to be particularly significant.

- What does line 244 suggest about the knight's expectations from marriage?

211-4	**And eek ... reste** [The reference to Wade's boat is obscure, but the sense is that old and experienced widows know too much trickery to let him have a peaceful life.]		pleasure with her, I would have to resort to adultery which would send me to Hell when I die
		225-8	**Ne children ... alle** Nor would I be able to father children on her and I would rather that hounds ate me than that strangers should inherit my property
215	**For sondry ... clerkis** many schools make a clever scholar [This is a proverb. January is suggesting that women who have experienced marriage are too clever at managing their husbands.]		
		229	**I dote nat** I'm not senile
		232	**my page** [Possibly a reference to Damyan, preparing the reader/audience for his appearance.]
216	**half a clerk is** is half-way to being a scholar		
		236	**leveful** lawful
217	**gye** direct or train	239	**eschue** renounce, avoid
218	**Right as ... plye** just as men can mould warm wax in their hands	240	**yelde hir dette** pay their debt [As part of the marriage contract each partner 'owed' the other sexual satisfaction.]
220-4	**I wol ... die** I won't have an old wife for this reason: if I should be so unlucky as not to find sexual		
		242	**meschief** misfortune

He tells his friends that older women, widows especially, know too much. He wants a young wife whom he may shape to his will, and who will bear him children.

And eek thise olde widwes, God it woot,
They konne so muchel craft on Wades boot,
So muchel broken harm, whan that hem leste,
That with hem sholde I nevere live in reste.
For sondry scoles maken sotile clerkis;   215
Womman of manye scoles half a clerk is.
But certeynly, a yong thing may men gye,
Right as men may warm wex with handes plye.
Wherfore I sey yow pleynly, in a clause,
I wol noon oold wyf han right for this cause.   220
For if so were I hadde swich mischaunce,
That I in hire ne koude han no plesaunce,
Thanne sholde I lede my lyf in avoutrye,
And go streight to the devel, whan I die.
Ne children sholde I none upon hire geten;   225
Yet were me levere houndes had me eten,
Than that myn heritage sholde falle
In straunge hand, and this I telle yow alle.
I dote nat, I woot the cause why
Men sholde wedde, and forthermoore woot I,   230
Ther speketh many a man of mariage
That woot namoore of it than woot my page,
For whiche causes man sholde take a wyf.
If he ne may nat liven chaast his lyf,
Take him a wyf with greet devocioun,   235
By cause of leveful procreacioun
Of children, to th'onour of God above,
And nat oonly for paramour or love;
And for they sholde leccherye eschue,
And yelde hir dette whan that it is due;   240
Or for that ech of hem sholde helpen oother
In meschief, as a suster shal the brother;
And live in chastitee ful holily.

29

- In groups of three, organise an improvisation in your own words on the advice given by the two brothers over the next three pages. Stay as close as you can to Chaucer's meaning. By giving them the names of 'Placebo' – I shall please, and 'Justinus' – the just one, Chaucer implies that January's brothers are types rather than individually realised characters. How does Placebo live up to his name in the speech that he makes to his brother?
- Look back at the section on Chaucer's language (page 8) and then read aloud lines 245-56, trying to get the rhythm right and paying particular attention to the pronunciation of the final 'e'.
- In lines 266-78 Placebo is suggesting that January is so wise that he does not need to take advice from his friends, but is doing so because he is wise enough to follow the judgements of Solomon. Consider how closely January follows his friends' advice as you read on.

245	**I dar make avaunt** I dare to boast that		257	**Diverse ... tolde** different men told him different things
246	**stark and suffisaunt** strong and satisfactory		261	**altercacioun** argument
250	**ywoxen** grown		262	**Bitwixen freendes in disputisoun** between friends in disagreement
251	**And blosmy ... deed** and a blossoming tree is neither dried up nor dead		267	**conseil to axe** to ask advice
			269	**sapience** wisdom, prudence
253-4	**Myn ... sene** my heart and all my limbs are as green as the laurel is all through the year [Laurel or bay is an evergreen tree.]		271	**weyven fro the word of Salomon** ignore the advice of Solomon [King Solomon is a king in the Old Testament who has a reputation for wisdom; he suggests seeking advice – see Ecclesiasticus 33.]
255-6	**And sin ... assente** and since you have all heard my plans, I hope that you'll all agree with me			

January goes on to say that he feels fit and strong enough for marriage, and he asks his friends what they think of his plan. Some of his friends agree with him and some disagree. His brother, Placebo, begins by flattering January and saying that with all his wisdom he scarcely needs to ask anyone else's advice.

But sires, by youre leve, that am nat I.
For, God by thanked, I dar make avaunt,   245
I feele my lymes stark and suffisaunt
To do al that a man bilongeth to;
I woot myselven best what I may do.
Though I be hoor, I fare as dooth a tree
That blosmeth er that fruit ywoxen bee;   250
And blosmy tree is neither drye ne deed.
I feele me nowhere hoor but on myn heed;
Myn herte and alle my lymes been as grene
As laurer thurgh the yeer is for to sene.
And sin that ye han herd al myn entente,   255
I prey yow to my wil ye wole assente.'
　　Diverse men diversely him tolde
Of mariage manye ensamples olde.
Somme blamed it, somme preysed it, certeyn;
But atte laste, shortly for to seyn,   260
As al day falleth altercacioun
Bitwixen freendes in disputisoun,
Ther fil a strif bitwixe his bretheren two,
Of whiche that oon was cleped Placebo,
Justinus soothly called was that oother.   265
　　Placebo seyde, 'O Januarie, brother,
Ful litel nede hadde ye, my lord so deere,
Conseil to axe of any that is heere,
But that ye been so ful of sapience
That yow ne liketh, for youre heighe prudence,   270
To weyven fro the word of Salomon.

- What might Placebo's flattery suggest about his relationship with January?
- Placebo's argument is that great lords are inherently wise because of their position. Do you think that this is true?
- In pairs, read this page aloud, taking it in turns to speak up to a punctuation mark. Aim to emphasise Placebo's personality by the way you speak the lines. What do you learn about him from this exercise? What have you noticed about the language?
- What do you think is the point of asking the advice of someone who is invariably going to agree with you?

273 **Wirk alle thing by conseil** do everything after taking advice

274 **shaltow** shalt thou (shall you)

275-8 **But though that ... is the beste** But though Solomon himself said this, my own dear lord and brother, I think your own opinion is best [See note for line 271 on Solomon.]

279 **of me taak this motif** take this advice from me

280 **court-man** courtier [but can also mean flatterer]

283 **in full greet degree** in a position of high status

285 **Yet hadde I nevere with noon of hem debaat** but I never argued with any of them

287 **ferme and stable** absolutely true

288 **semblable** similar

292 **his conseil sholde passe his lordes wit** his advice is better than his lord's judgement

295 **So heigh sentence** such good judgement

296 **Ne in Itaille** nor in Italy

300 **halt him** considers him
    apaid satisfied

Placebo gives his judgement first. He tells his brother to trust his own opinion and not to rely on the advice of others. Placebo says that, like any good adviser, he would never presume to contradict a lord's opinion.

This word seyde he unto us everychon:
"Wirk alle thing by conseil," thus seyde he,
"And thanne shaltow not repente thee."
But though that Salomon spak swich a word,   275
Myn owene deere brother and my lord,
So wisly God my soule bringe at reste,
I holde youre owene conseil is the beste.
For, brother myn, of me taak this motif,
I have now been a court-man al my lyf,   280
And God it woot, though I unworthy be,
I have stonden in ful greet degree
Abouten lordes of ful heigh estaat;
Yet hadde I nevere with noon of hem debaat.
I nevere hem contraried, trewely;   285
I woot wel that my lord kan moore than I.
With that he seith, I holde it ferme and stable;
I seye the same, or elles thing semblable.
A ful greet fool is any conseillour
That serveth any lord of heigh honour,   290
That dar presume, or elles thenken it,
That his conseil sholde passe his lordes wit.
Nay, lordes been no fooles, by my fay.
Ye han youreselven shewed heer to-day
So heigh sentence, so holily and weel,   295
That I consente and conferme everydeel
Youre wordes alle and youre opinioun.
By God, ther nis no man in al this toun,
Ne in Itaille, that koude bet han said!
Crist halt him of this conseil ful wel apaid.   300

- Placebo's final lines take the discussion no further forward. In effect he says – do what you want, that's best. What is the effect of this advice at this point?
- Look again at lines 320-4. How many qualities of good women does Justinus mention, and how many vices? What does this add to your understanding of his character? Write four similar lines that caution a woman who is choosing a husband.

301	**an heigh courage** a brave deed		314	**sin** since
302	**stapen is in age** is in advanced old age [*literally:* stepped far in age]		319	**avisement** considering carefully
			321	**dronkelewe** a drunkard
303	**my fader kin** ancestors		323	**chidestere** nagging woman
304	**Youre herte hangeth on a joly pin!** You've got a merry heart! [with a connotation of sexuality]		324	**mannissh wood** man-mad
			326	**trotteth hool in al** perfect in every way [The use of the word 'trotting' makes it sound as if he is buying a horse rather than marrying a wife.]
307	**that ay ... herde** who had continued to sit still and listen			
312	**oghte him right wel avise** ought to consider very carefully		330	**mo** more
				thewes manners
313	**yeveth** gives		331	**leyser** leisure, time
	catel goods			

Placebo agrees with January that it is a good idea for any elderly man to marry a young wife. Justinus disagrees. He thinks that a man should be careful about giving away his property, and that marriage needs a great deal of thought.

And trewely, it is an heigh corage
Of any man that stapen is in age
To take a yong wif; by my fader kin,
Youre herte hangeth on a joly pin!
Dooth now in this matiere right as yow leste, 305
For finally I holde it for the beste.'
   Justinus, that ay stille sat and herde,
Right in this wise he to Placebo answerde:
'Now, brother myn, be pacient, I preye,
Sin ye han seyd, and herkneth what I seye. 310
Senek, amonges othere wordes wise,
Seith that a man oghte him right wel avise
To whom he yeveth his lond or his catel.
And sin I oghte avise me right wel
To whom I yeve my good awey fro me, 315
Wel muchel moore I oghte avised be
To whom I yeve my body for alwey.
I warne yow wel, it is no childes pley
To take a wyf withouten avisement.
Men moste enquere, this is myn assent, 320
Wher she be wys, or sobre, or dronkelewe,
Or proud, or elles ootherweys a shrewe,
A chidestere, or wastour of thy good,
Or riche, or poore, or elles mannissh wood.
Al be it so that no man finden shal 325
Noon in this world that trotteth hool in al,
Ne man, ne beest, swich as men koude devise;
But nathelees it oghte ynough suffise
With any wyf, if so were that she hadde
Mo goode thewes than hire vices badde; 330
And al this axeth leyser for t'enquere.

- Is Placebo right? Is it worth arguing with someone who has already made up their mind?
- What about Justinus? How would you describe his advice, taking account of his possible motives for giving it in these circumstances?
- Look back at the Prologue to the Merchant's Tale. Do Justinus' views have anything in common with those of the Merchant himself?
- Justinus' view are not what January wants to hear. Read lines 354-9 aloud. How does Chaucer help you to convey the appropriate tone?

334 **Preyse whoso wole a wedded mannes lyf** I don't care who praises the life of a married man

335-6 **Certein I finde ... bare** Certainly I only find expense and worry and duties, with no pleasures at all

338 **namely of wommen many a route** particularly by many women

339 **stedefast** faithful

340 **mekeste** most humble (most meek)
bereth lyf alive

341 **But I woot best where wringeth me my sho** I know best where my shoe pinches

342 **Aviseth yow** think very carefully

347 **route** company

348 **bisy ynough** has enough to do
bringen it aboute manage

349 **han his wyf allone** have his wife to himself

352 **an observaunce** attentions

353 **yvele apaid** displeased

355 **Straw for thy Senek, and for thy proverbes!** I don't give a straw for Seneca or for your sayings!

356-7 **I counte nat a panyer ful of herbes of scole-termes** your philosophy (scholastic sayings) is not worth a basket of herbs

361 **That letteth matrimoigne, sikerly** who hinders marriage, certainly

Justinus tells January that he is speaking from experience. Though his friends think that his wife is faithful and meek, he knows how she has made him suffer in private. He suggests that January think more carefully before marrying a young wife. January rejects his advice and turns back to Placebo whose advice is more agreeable.

For, God it woot, I have wept many a teere
Ful prively, sin I have had a wyf.
Preyse whoso wole a wedded mannes lyf,
Certein I finde in it but cost and care   335
And observances, of alle blisses bare.
And yet, God woot, my neighebores aboute,
And namely of wommen many a route,
Seyn that I have the mooste stedefast wyf,
And eek the mekeste oon that bereth lyf;   340
But I woot best where wringeth me my sho.
Ye mowe, for me, right as yow liketh do;
Aviseth yow—ye been a man of age—
How that ye entren into mariage,
And namely with a yong wyf and a fair.   345
By him that made water, erthe, and air,
The yongeste man that is in al this route
Is bisy ynough to bringen it aboute
To han his wyf allone. Trusteth me,
Ye shul nat plesen hire fully yeres thre,—   350
This is to seyn, to doon hire ful plesaunce.
A wif axeth ful many an observaunce.
I prey yow that ye be nat yvele apaid.'
   'Wel,' quod this Januarie, 'and hastow said?
Straw for thy Senek, and for thy proverbes!   355
I counte nat a panyer ful of herbes
Of scole-termes. Wiser men than thow,
As thou hast herd, assenteden right now
To my purpos. Placebo, what sey ye?'
   'I seye it is a cursed man,' quod he,   360
'That letteth matrimoigne, sikerly.'

37

- What do you think is the point of the debate between January's brothers? He has encouraged them only to agree with him. Some people think that we only ask advice from those whom we expect will tell us to do what we want to do. Organise a debate on the motion: This house believes that asking advice is a waste of time.
- What do you think is Chaucer's motive in giving his audience a debate on such matters before the story really begins?
- The whole extended image of January setting up a mental mirror in a market place (line 370) reinforces the suggestion that there is a lack of solid substance in his selection of a bride. Given that Chaucer uses the image of a market place, what view of the transaction does this give?
- In lines 377-81 Chaucer seems to suggest that January is spoilt for choice. What do you think of the qualities he mentions as a basis for choosing a marriage partner? In fact, are not all the arguments for and against marriage really a distortion of the ideals associated with it? Words like 'love' and 'fidelity' seem to have been left out. Discuss other viewpoints and attitudes that Chaucer is inviting his audience to consider as they read these biased and distorted opinions.

363-4	**And been ... where he wolde** and they agreed that he should marry when and where he wished	376	**wiste nat wher that he mighte abide** did not know which to settle on
365-7	**Heigh fantasye ... aboute his mariage** intense imagination and constant thoughts of marriage became increasingly fixed in January's mind	382	**bitwixe ernest and game** between seriousness and joking
		383	**apointed him on oon** chose one
		385	**chees** chose
368	**shap** figure		**auctoritee** authority
	visage face	386	**love is blind** [The image of Cupid as the blind young god of love is traditional. In this story, the image becomes a physical reality that reflects the spiritual and ethical blindness that is already becoming evident to the audience.]
370	**mirour** mirror		
373	**wise** way		
374	**inwith** in		
375	**biside** nearby		
			alday always

January's brothers finally agree that he should get married as he wishes. He begins to consider
choosing a wife, eventually deciding on a suitable maiden.

And with that word they risen sodeynly,
And been assented fully that he sholde
Be wedded whanne him liste, and where he wolde.
   Heigh fantasye and curious bisynesse 365
Fro day to day gan in the soule impresse
Of Januarie about his mariage.
Many fair shap and many a fair visage
Ther passeth thurgh his herte night by night,
As whoso tooke a mirour, polisshed bright, 370
And sette it in a commune market-place,
Thanne sholde he se ful many a figure pace
By his mirour: and in the same wise
Gan Januarie inwith his thoght devise
Of maidens whiche that dwelten him biside. 375
He wiste nat wher that he mighte abide.
For if that oon have beaute in hir face,
Another stant so in the peples grace
For hire sadnesse and hire beningnitee
That of the peple grettest voys hath she; 380
And somme were riche, and hadden badde name.
But nathelees, bitwixe ernest and game,
He atte laste apointed him on oon,
And leet alle othere from his herte goon,
And chees hire of his owene auctoritee; 385
For love is blind alday, and may nat see.

- January fantasises about the kind of young woman he wishes to marry. What impression do you gain from this insight into January's thoughts?
- Do you find January admirable for choosing a bride without reference to her financial or social status?
- 'Governaunce' and 'gentillesse' are two qualities much valued in Chaucer's day. As you read on, bear them in mind and consider whether these are indeed qualities possessed by his bride. Discuss with a partner how much January actually knows about his chosen bride, and how much is just his 'fantasy'.
- Read lines 387-389 aloud, aiming to express the thoughts and feelings expressed.
- What is it that January admires in the bride he would like to marry?

387   **whan ... his bed ybroght** when his servants had attended him to bed

388   **purtreyed** imagined

390   **Hir middel smal, hire armes longe and sklendre** her slim waist and her long slender arms

391   **governaunce** self-possession, self-control

      gentillesse good breeding, nobility of character

392   **beringe** conduct [with overtones of traditional feminine qualities of chastity and loyalty]

      sadnesse serious manner

393   **was condescended** had fixed his choice

394   **Him thoughte ... ben amended** he thought that no-one could improve on his choice ['Choys' here means both his decision, and the girl that he has chosen.]

397-8   **repplye Again** criticise

398   **this was his fantasye** [Because he is attracted to her, he values her by his image of her.]

402-4   **He wolde abregge ... he wolde abide** he would shorten their tasks. They had no more need to search for a bride for him; he had made his choice and would stick to it

406   **alderfirst ... prosperitee** first of all he asked them a favour: that none would make any objections. His choice pleased God and was the true ground of his good fortune [Now that January has made up his mind, he is not interested in the opinions of his friends.]

413-4   **Al were it ... hir beautee** although she came from a humble family, he finds her youth and beauty sufficient for him

He has fantasies about his chosen bride and considers that he has made the best possible decision.
He calls his friends to hear about his choice but forbids them to disagree with him. He has chosen a
beautiful young maiden in the town, though she is not from a family of high status.

And whan that he was in his bed ybroght,
He purtreyed in his herte and in his thoght
Hir fresshe beautee and hir age tendre,
Hir middel smal, hire armes longe and sklendre,   390
Hir wise governaunce, hir gentillesse,
Hir wommanly beringe, and hire sadnesse.
And whan that he on hire was condescended,
Him thoughte his choys mighte nat ben amended.
For whan that he himself concluded hadde,   395
Him thoughte ech oother mannes wit so badde
That inpossible it were to repplye
Again his choys, this was his fantasye.
His freendes sente he to, at his instaunce,
And preyed hem to doon him that plesaunce,   400
That hastily they wolden to him come;
He wolde abregge hir labour, alle and some.
Nedeth namoore for hem to go ne ride;
He was apointed ther he wolde abide.
    Placebo cam, and eek his freendes soone,   405
And alderfirst he bad hem alle a boone,
That noon of hem none argumentes make
Again the purpos which that he hath take,
Which purpos was plesant to God, seyde he,
And verray ground of his prosperitee.   410
    He seyde ther was a maiden in the toun,
Which that of beautee hadde greet renoun,
Al were it so she were of smal degree;
Suffiseth him hir yowthe and hir beautee.

- Notice Chaucer's clear insistence on January's understanding of theological doctrine, lines 425-42. He knows that the church teaches that suffering on earth can be rewarded by heaven. He is hoping for two heavens; one of them being on earth with his young wife. How do these fears lead you to respond to January's personality here? With sympathy? Or contempt? Or what?
- Given that January has already rejected the advice given by his friends and forbidden them to comment on his choice of bride, why do you think that he is asking their counsel again? Before you read on, note your predictions of what their advice might be.

416	**to lede in ese and hoolinesse his lyf** to lead his life in ease and blessedness [reinforces the suggestions of moral ambiguity]
417	**he mighte han hire al** he could wholly possess her
418	**no wight his blisse parten shal** no one will diminish his joy
419	**preyed hem** asked them **nede** moment of need
423	**o thing priketh** one thing disturbs
424	**reherce** speak about
425	**ful yoore ago** long ago
426	**Ther may no man han parfite blesses two** no man may experience perfect happiness twice
428	**sinnes sevene** the seven deadly sins

429	**thilke tree** this tree [The seven deadly sins were frequently depicted in the shape of a tree in medieval art.]
430	**felicitee** happiness
432	**agast** terrified
434	**so delicat** so much to my taste
437	**penaunce** suffering in payment for sins committed
438	**How sholde I ... eterne on live is?** then how should I, who will be living in such pleasure as all married men do with their wives, go to heaven where Christ lives eternally?
442	**assoilleth** explain, answer

'For though he kepe him fro the sinnes sevene,
And eek from every branche of thilke tree ...'

42

He tells his friends that there is only one thing that now disturbs him. He has heard that men cannot experience perfect bliss twice, and as all married men have perfect joy with their wives, how will he achieve heaven when he is dead?

Which maide, he seyde, he wolde han to his wyf, 415
To lede in ese and hoolinesse his lyf;
And thanked God that he mighte han hire al,
That no wight his blisse parten shal.
And preyed hem to laboure in this nede,
And shapen that he faille nat to spede; 420
For thanne, he seyde, his spirit was at ese.
'Thanne is, quod he, 'no thing may me displese,
Save o thing priketh in my conscience,
The which I wol reherce in youre presence.
    I have,' quod he, 'herd seyd, ful yoore ago, 425
Ther may no man han parfite blisses two—
This is to seye, in erthe and eek in hevene.
For though he kepe him fro the sinnes sevene,
And eek from every branche of thilke tree,
Yet is ther so parfit felicitee 430
And so greet ese and lust in mariage,
That evere I am agast now in myn age
That I shal lede now so myrie a lyf,
So delicat, withouten wo and stryf,
That I shal have myn hevene in erthe heere. 435
For sith that verray hevene is boght so deere
With tribulacion and greet penaunce,
How sholde I thanne, that live in swich plesaunce
As alle wedded men doon with hire wyvys,
Come to the blisse ther Crist eterne on live is? 440
This is my drede, and ye, my bretheren tweye,
Assoilleth me this question, I preye.'

Purgatory is believed to be a place or time of punishment after death. Unlike Hell, where punishment for sins committed in life was eternal, Purgatory was a place of purification through suffering, with the prospect of Heaven at some time in the future. The pilgrims have already heard from the Wife of Bath who has frankly told them that she acted as purgatory for one of her husbands: 'By God, in erthe I was his purgatorie/ For which I hope his soule be in glorie'. There seems to be a direct reference to the Wife of Bath by Justinus in lines 458-9, reinforcing this link.

• Read Justinus' advice aloud. How does Chaucer convey the tone of Justinus' advice through his manner of offering it?

443   **folye** foolishness

444   **Answerde anon right in his japerye** answered mockingly straightaway

445   **abbregge** shorten (abridge)

446   **He wolde noon auctoritee allegge** he wouldn't cite any authority

449   **wirche** work

450   **er ye have youre right of hooly chirche** before you die [*literally:* before you receive your last rites from the church]

453   **elles** otherwise
     sente should send

455   **wel ofte** more often

456   **the beste reed I kan** the best advice I know

457   **Dispeire yow noght** don't despair

458   **paraunter** perhaps

459   **meene** instrument

460   **Thanne shal youre soule up to hevene skippe** [The image of January's soul skipping up to heaven suggests a very brisk and happy departure from life after a miserable marriage.]

461   **arwe** arrow

463-5   **That ther nis no ... savacion** marriage is not so happy that it will prevent you receiving salvation [Justinus is being very forthright in his warnings about the lack of perfect happiness in marriage.]

466   **skile** care

467   **lustes** pleasures
     attemprely within reason [January is being reminded that even within marriage the church did not condone too much indulgence in carnal pleasures.]

470   **doon** finished, ended

471   **Beth not agast herof** don't be frightened by my words

472   **But let us waden out of this mateere** let's leave the subject

Justinus tells him not to worry. God would not allow a married man less chance of heaven than a single man. In any case, he says, it may happen that his wife will serve as January's purgatory on earth, then he would be able to go straight to heaven when he dies.

Justinus, which that hated his folye,
Answerde anon right in his japerye;
And for he wolde his longe tale abregge,   445
He wolde noon auctoritee allegge,
But seyde, 'Sire, so ther be noon obstacle
Oother than this, God of his high miracle
And of his mercy may so for yow wirche
That, er ye have youre right of hooly chirche,   450
Ye may repente of wedded mannes lyf,
In which ye seyn ther is no wo ne stryf.
And elles, God forbede but he sente
A wedded man him grace to repente
Wel ofte rather than a sengle man.   455
And therfore, sire–the beste reed I kan–
Dispeire yow noght, but have in youre memorie,
Paraunter she may be youre purgatorie.
She may be Goddes meene and Goddes whippe;
Thanne shal youre soule up to hevene skippe   460
Swifter than dooth an arwe out of a bowe.
I hope to God, herafter shul ye knowe
That ther nis no so greet felicitee
In mariage, ne nevere mo shal bee,
That yow shal lette of youre savacion,   465
So that ye use, as skile is and reson,
The lustes of youre wyf attemprely,
And that ye plese hire nat to amorously,
And that ye kepe yow eek from oother sinne.
My tak is doon, for my wit is thinne.   470
Beth nat agast herof, my brother deere,
But lat us waden out of this mateere.

- When Justinus refers to the Wife of Bath explicitly, it is an anomaly. She is part of the pilgrimage to Canterbury and so has no place in an individual story. (For more information about the Wife of Bath's Prologue and Tale, and its relationship to the Merchant's Prologue and Tale see page 108.)
- Talk together about which of the following seems the most likely explanation: a) Chaucer has slipped up; b) Chaucer is implying that the Wife is so well known that even the characters in the story have heard of her; c) Chaucer wishes to give the impression that the Merchant gets so involved in his anti-marriage story that he reminds the audience of the Wife of Bath and the way that she treated her husbands; d) Chaucer is playing a joke on those readers who believe the events of the tale to be true, as a fictional character is not limited to factual possibility. Chaucer can write them both into his story, just as an artist could draw them in the same picture.
- There has been a long and detailed debate about whether January should marry, and the benefits of marriage, but once the decision has been made, he rushes to conclude the wedding. Look at lines 479-97. Read them over carefully aloud and note all the ways in which Chaucer emphasises the haste of the marriage arrangements.

474 **have on honde** are concerned with

475 **in litel space** briefly [This must be ironic. The Wife of Bath has an unusually long prologue in which she details her abuse of her five husbands.]

477-8 **And with this word ... of oother** so saying, Justinus and his brother took leave of January and of everyone else

479 **saugh that it moste nedes be** understood that it was inevitable

480 **wroghten** worked

tretee negotiation

481 **which that Mayus highte** who was called May [suggesting Springtime and youth. Her name is mentioned for the first time at this late stage reinforcing the idea that her identity is not very important. We still know almost nothing about her.]

485 **scrit and bond** writ and bond [legal documents concerned with the purchase of land]

486 **feffed in his lond** endowed with his land [The impression given by the legal terms, 'feffed', 'scrit' and 'bond' is that May has been bought.]

487 **array** clothing, garments

491 **stole** [part of the vestments of the priest, a long narrow piece of material worn over his shoulders when he takes a service]

492 **lyk Sarra and Rebekke** [One of the prayers often used at weddings is that the bride should be as wise as Rebecca and as long-lived and faithful as Sarah – but see page 24 on Rebecca.]

494 **And seyde his orisons, as is usage** and said his prayers, as is customary [Even the priest doesn't sound very devout.]

495 **croucheth hem** made the sign of the Cross over them

496 **And made al siker ynough with hoolinesse** and made the marriage binding with religion [The language suggests a sticking plaster, or an insurance policy.]

Justinus refers January back to the Wife of Bath's account of her five marriages, then leaves him.
January's friends help to arrange the marriage contract as swiftly as possible. January and his bride
are married in church.

The Wyf of Bathe, if ye han understonde,
Of mariage, which we have on honde,
Declared hath ful wel in litel space.   475
Fareth now wel, God have yow in his grace.'
    And with this word this Justin and his brother
Han take hir leve, and ech of hem of oother.
For whan they saughe that it moste nedes be,
They wroghten so, by sly and wys tretee,   480
That she, this maiden, which that Mayus highte,
As hastily as evere that she mighte,
Shal wedded be unto this Januarie.
I trowe it were to longe yow to tarie,
If I yow tolde of every scrit and bond   485
By which that she was feffed in his lond,
Or for to herknen of hir riche array.
But finally ycomen is the day
That to the chirche bothe be they went
For to receyve the hooly sacrement.   490
Forth comth the preest, with stole aboute his nekke,
And bad hire be lyk Sarra and Rebekke
In wisdom and in trouthe of mariage;
And seyde his orisons, as is usage,
And croucheth hem, and bad God sholde hem blesse,   495
And made al siker ynogh with hoolinesse.

'... this maiden, which that Mayus highte,
As hastily as evere that she mighte,
Shal wedded be unto this Januarie'

Orpheus, Amphion, Joab and Theodomas were all famous men from classical and biblical stories who were also renowned for their ability to make music.

- The description of the wedding feast and the music accompanying it is very elaborate and detailed, especially when compared with the rushed description of the actual wedding. The elaborate ceremony and sophistication of the classical references also form a strong contrast to the down-to-earth description of the wedding night that follows. What aspects of this marriage are emphasised by the specific details that Chaucer chooses to include?
- Think of a way of representing the feast of January and May. You could make a group tableau of one moment of the feast, or draw a picture, or write a piece for the *Lombardy Times*.
- Lines 526-7 are the essence of the poem: the contrast between the adjectives 'tendre' and 'stouping' is very marked and reveals the inappropriate match. And does the indescribable 'swich mirthe' mean such joy, or such amusement for the reader?

499	**deys** dais, platform [The raised floor at the end of the hall where the most important people sat at table.]	511	**Venus** the goddess of carnal love **wight** person
500	**paleys** palace [The description of the feast begins with a reminder of January's wealth.]	513-4	**assayen his corage In libertee, and eek in mariage** try his sexual prowess in promiscuity and also in marriage
501	**vitaille** food	515-6	[Venus is described as leading the dance with her flaming torch, symbolising passion.]
502	**the mooste deyntevous of al Itaille** the finest in all Italy		
503-5	**Biforn hem stoode ... a melodye** the instruments played for them were even more melodious than those of Orpheus or Amphion of Thebes	516	**al the route** all the company
		518	**Ymeneus, that god of wedding is** Hymen, who is the god of marriage
		519	**myrie** merry
506	**At every cours thanne cam loud minstralcye** music plays at every course of the banquet	520-4	**Hoold thou thy pees ... mariage** be silent, Marcian, you who write of the merry wedding of Philology and Mercury, and of the songs of the Muses [a reference to a classical work by Marcianus Capella]
510	**Bacus the wyn hem shinketh al aboute** Bacchus (the god of wine) pours wine for them all [Notice the way that the Christian sacrament of marriage has become a pagan celebration.]	528	**assayeth** try it **witen** know

The wedding feast is very elaborate. There is music for every course at the banquet. This wedding exceeds the famous description of the wedding of Philology and Mercury in the poem by Martianus Capella.

Thus been they wedded with solempnitee
And at the feeste sitteth he and she
With othere worthy folk upon the deys.
Al ful of joye and blisse is the paleys,   500
And ful of instrumentz and of vitaille,
The mooste deyntevous of al Itaille:
Biforn hem stoode instrumentz of swich soun
That Orpheus, ne of Thebes Amphioun,
Ne maden nevere swich a melodye.   505
At every cours thanne cam loud minstralcye,
That nevere tromped Joab for to heere,
Nor he Theodomas, yet half so cleere,
At Thebes, whan the citee was in doute.
Bacus the wyn hem shinketh al aboute,   510
And Venus laugheth upon every wight,
For Januarie was bicome hir knight,
And wolde bothe assayen his corage
In libertee, and eek in mariage;
And with hire fyrbrond in hire hand aboute   515
Daunceth biforn the bride and al the route,
And certeinly, I dar right wel seyn this,
Ymeneus, that god of wedding is,
Saugh nevere his lyf so myrie a wedded man.
Hoold thou thy pees, thou poete Marcian,   520
That writest us that like wedding murie
Of hire Philologie and him Mercurie,
And of the songes that the Muses songe.
To smal is bothe thy penne, and eek thy tonge.
For to descriven of this mariage: 525
Whan tendre youthe hath wedded stouping age,
Ther is swich mirthe that it may nat be writen.
Assayeth it youreself, thanne may ye witen
If that I lie or noon in this matiere.

In line 542 the Merchant refers to the story of Paris and Helen. Helen was the wife of a Greek leader, Menelaus, and Paris was a young prince of Troy who abducted her. This precipitated the Trojan war. This is a popular story where the protagonists are stereotypes: Paris, young noble lover; Helen, supremely beautiful woman (or whore); Menelaus, foolish cuckolded old husband. In his imagination January sees himself as Paris; the reader might see him as Menelaus.

- What do you think of January's violent fantasies about May? One student suggested, 'It shows Chaucer's realism – all men have thoughts about aggressive lovemaking. It doesn't mean they are all potential rapists. Anyway he redeems himself when he shows concern for how she will endure their first night'. What do you think?
- Read lines 538-51 in pairs, changing speaker at each punctuation mark. What do you notice about the sentence structure, rhyme and rhythm? Talk about the impression that you think Chaucer intends the reader to receive.

530	**so beningne a chiere** such a meek expression
531	**faierye** enchanting ['like something from the fairy world' enhances the idea of a fantasy wife]
532-3	[King Ahasuerus was charmed by Esther's meekness and beauty. However she also looked meek when she was plotting the death of Haman.]
534	**devise** describe
536	**the brighte morwe of May** a brilliant morning in May [Just as January's name is emblematic of winter, May's symbolises youth.]
538	**ravisshed in a traunce** gets carried away in a trance, or fantasy

540	**But in his herte he gan hire to manace** in his imagination he began to menace or threaten her
541	**streyne** clasp tightly
547	**corage** sexual desire
	keene eager
548	**agast** afraid
549	**But God forbede that I did al my might!** But God forbid that I should make love with all my energy. [January has a high opinion of his own virility.]
550-1	**Now wolde God that it were woxen night** I wish to God that it was night-time
555	**fro the mete in subtil wise** from the feast tactfully

May, the bride of January, sits calmly – looking young and beautiful. Every time January looks at her he feels enraptured and begins to fantasise about the coming night. He is desperate for the wedding guests to leave, and tries to hurry them through the meal tactfully.

Mayus, that sit with so beningne a chiere,   530
Hire to biholde it semed faierye.
Queene Ester looked nevere with swich an ye
On Assuer, so meke a look hath she.
I may yow nat devise al hir beautee.
But thus muche of hire beautee telle I may,   535
That she was lyk the brighte morwe of May,
Fulfild of alle beautee and plesaunce.
     This Januarie is ravisshed in a traunce
At every time he looked on hir face;
But in his herte he gan hire to manace   540
That he that night in armes wolde hire streyne
Harder than evere Paris dide Eleyne.
But nathelees yet hadde he greet pitee
That thilke night offenden hire moste he,
And thoughte, 'Allas, O tendre creature,   545
Now wolde God ye mighte wel endure
Al my corage, it is so sharp and keene.
I am agast ye shul it nat susteene.
But God forbede that I dide al my might!
Now wolde God that it were woxen night,   550
And that the night wolde lasten everemo.
I wolde that al this peple were ago.'
And finally he dooth al his labour,
As he best mighte, savinge his honour,
To haste hem fro the mete in subtil wise.   555

- If you have sufficient people, create a frozen image of the wedding feast with January and May and their honoured guests at the top table, served by Damyan. He is struck by Venus' flaming torch and falls instantly and painfully in love with May.
- Read aloud lines 562-5 and pick out all the words that describe the violent physical pain of falling in love. Do you think that Damyan's feelings about May differ significantly from January's?
- Lines 571-5 are a rhetorical device called an apostrophe. This is when the poet addresses something/one in a declamatory way, often signalled by 'O . . .'. Try writing your own apostrophe on the subject of betrayal. Look particularly at Chaucer's use of imagery here: fire breeding in the straw used for stuffing mattresses, is an aptly intimate and domestic image for January's betrayal by his favourite servant. Attempt to capture the same gleeful anticipation of disaster that Chaucer achieves here.

556 **The time cam that resoun was to rise** when it was the appropriate time they rose from the banquet

560 **al but** except for [Is this the true servant of line 86?]

561 **Which carf biforn the knight** who carved and served the meat to the knight [The phrase 'carf biforn' echoes the description of the close relationship between the Knight and the Squire in the General Prologue. Damyan is a trusted household servant.]

562 **ravisshed** enraptured

563 **verray peyne** true pain (of love)

ny wood almost mad

564 **swelte and swowned ther he stood** fainted and swooned on the spot [Damyan is as much of a fantasiser as his master. He too desires an image. We shall see later on whether or not May is as lovely spiritually and emotionally.]

568 **namoore** no more

569 **pleyne** complain

570 **rewen on his peyne** will take pity on his suffering [a hint of the plot thickening later]

572 **famulier foo** false friend, who treacherously offers his services

572-3 **bedeth ... false hoomly hewe** ['hewe' and 'servant' mean the same. The repetition is deliberate.]

574 **naddre** adder [The comparison of Damyan to the adder is striking after January's insistence on the married state as being an earthly paradise. Chaucer now brings in the inevitable serpent to tempt the woman.]

576 **dronken in plesaunce** In mariage drunk with the lustful delights of marriage

578 **thy borne man** a man born on your estate

579 **Entendeth for to do thee vileynye** intends to do you harm

580 **God graunte thee thyn hoomly fo t'espye** God give you grace to see what your enemy in the household is doing. [With a probable reference to January regaining his sight at the end of the Tale.]

Eventually the feast ended with everyone full of merriment except for January's squire, Damyan, who has been struck by love for May, so much so that he leaves the feast and goes to bed. The Merchant warns his audience about danger coming from within the home.

The time cam that resoun was to rise;
And after that men daunce and drinken faste,
And spices al aboute the hous they caste;
And ful of joye and blisse is every man,—
Al but a squier, highte Damyan,   560
Which carf biforn the knight ful many a day.
He was so ravisshed on his lady May
That for the verray peyne he was ny wood.
Almoost he swelte and swowned ther he stood,
So soore hath Venus hurt him with hire brond,   565
As that she bar it daunsinge in hire hond;
And to his bed he wente him hastily.
Namoore of him as at this time speke I,
But there I lete him wepe ynogh and pleyne,
Til fresshe May wol rewen on his peyne.   570
    O perilous fyr, that in the bedstraw bredeth;
O famulier foo, that his service bedeth;
O servant traitour, false hoomly hewe,
Lyk to the naddre in bosom sly untrewe,
God shilde us alle from youre aqueyntaunce,
O Januarie, dronken in plesaunce
In mariage, se how thy Damyan,
Thyn owene squier and thy borne man,
Entendeth for to do thee vileynye.
God graunte thee thyn hoomly fo t'espye.
For in this world nis worse pestilence
Than hoomly foo al day in thy presence.

- Chaucer gives the Merchant a very poetic way of describing nightfall. It is striking because it seems almost redundant in the description of January's haste to get rid of his guests and get May to bed. Why do you think this might be? Is he trying to cover the indecent scramble with a cloak of respectability? Or ironically drawing attention to it? Try writing your own description of dusk or dawn in iambic pentameter.
- Constantinus Afer wrote a book called *de Coitu* in the eleventh century. This was a book of advice on sexual intercourse and prescribed various treatments for male problems, especially impotence. Why do you think Chaucer has the Merchant call Constantine 'cursed' in line 598? Why might he suggest that the Merchant has detailed knowledge of his advice? What irony does this add to the Tale? How do lines 595-600 provide an ironic contrast to his anxieties for his bride in lines 443-448?
- What impression of the bridal night do you think Chaucer intends the reader to have when he describes May as 'stille as stoon'?

583	**Parfourned hath the sonne his ark diurne** the sun has completed his daily arc
585	**on th'orisonte** on the horizon
586	**mantel** cloak
587	**Gan oversprede the hemisperie aboute** began to cover half the world
588	**lusty route** pleasant company
590	**lustily** cheerfully
593	**hastif** impatient
595-6	**he drinketh ypocras …t'encreessen his corage** [January drinks aphrodisiacs to increase his sexual potency. **Ypocras** is spiced wine, **clarree** is wine mixed with honey and spices, and **vernage** is strong Italian wine. These are all recommended in Constantinus Afer's book.]
597	**letuarie** remedy

598	**cursed** [the Merchant's term not, significantly, January's]
600	**To eten hem alle he nas no thing eschu** he was not averse to trying them all
601	**privee freendes** personal friends
603	**Lat voiden al this hous in curteys wise** clear out of the house discreetly
605	**the travers drawe anon** the bed curtains were drawn straight away
606	**The bride was broght abedde as stille as stoon** [Convention decreed the bride was escorted to the bridal bed.]
607	**with the preest yblessed** blessed by the priest
608	**Out of the chambre hath every wight him dressed** everyone else left the room

When the sun goes down the guests leave. January is in a hurry to get to bed, so he encourages his closest friends to leave quickly. May is brought to his bed.

Parfourned hath the sonne his ark diurne;
No lenger may the body of him sojurne
On th'orisonte, as in that latitude.   585
Night with his mantel, that is derk and rude,
Gan oversprede the hemisperie aboute;
For which departed is this lusty route
Fro Januarie, with thank on every side.
Hoom to hir houses lustily they ride,   590
Where as they doon hir thinges as hem leste,
And whan they sye hir time, goon to reste,
Soone after that, this hastif Januarie
Wolde go to bedde, he wolde no lenger tarye,
He drinketh ypocras, clarree, and vernage   595
Of spices hoote, t'encreessen his corage;
And many a letuarie hath he ful fyn,
Swiche as the cursed monk, daun Constantin,
Hath writen in his book *De Coitu*;
To eten hem alle he nas no thing eschu.   600
And to his privee freendes thus seyde he:
'For Goddes love, as soone as it may be,
Lat voiden al this hous in curteys wise.'
And they han doon right as he wol devise,
Men drinken, and the travers drawe anon.   605
The bride was broght abedde as stille as stoon;
And whan the bed was with the preest yblessed,
Out of the chambre hath every wight him dressed;

At the time older men wore beards, only young men tended to be clean-shaven. Possibly January is making on extra effort to appear young by having himself shaved, though 'in his manere' (line 614) can mean 'as was his habit'.

- Chaucer rhymes 'wyf' with 'knyf' (lines 627-8) when saying that a man can't sin with his own wife, nor harm himself with his own knife. Do you think that this is true? What effect does the rhyme have here?
- What is your opinion of his cheerful singing? Do you find it a natural expression of joy after successful lovemaking? Or does Chaucer's depiction of the loose skin on his neck shaking while he croaks out his song destroy the moment of joy? Does this eager love make him seem pitiable or despicable to you?

610   **his make** his marriage partner, mate

611   **lulleth** caressed

613   **skin of houndfissh** dogfish skin [often used as sandpaper by carpenters]

       brere briar

614   **shave al newe** freshly shaved

616   **moot trespace** must do wrong to you

618   **Er time come that I wil doun descende** before I go to sleep [also a sexual innuendo]

620-1   **Ther nis no werkman ... werke wel and hastily** no workman, whoever he is, can do his best in haste

622   **parfitly** perfectly

623   **It is no fors how longe that we pleye** it doesn't matter how long we enjoy ourselves

624   **tweye** two

629   **leve** permission

630   **laboureth he til that the day gan dawe** he worked hard until the day began to dawn

631   **sop in fyn clarree** bread dipped in wine [not an unusual early breakfast]

634   **wantown cheere** wantonness, lechery

635   **al coltissh, ful of ragerye** frisky as a colt

636   **jargon as a flekked pye** chatter as a spotted magpie [Note the animal imagery.]

638   **craketh** croaked

January takes May in his arms, apologises for the potential violence of his embraces. He says that he will take his time over making love to her like a skilful workman. At dawn he sings, triumphantly.

And Januarie hath faste in armes take
His fresshe May, his paradis, his make.   610
He lulleth hire, he kisseth hire ful ofte;
With thikke brustles of his berd unsofte,
Lyk to the skin of houndfissh, sharp as brere—
For he was shave al newe in his manere—
He rubbeth hire aboute hir tendre face,   615
And seyde thus, 'Allas, I moot trespace
To yow, my spouse, and yow greetly offende,
Er time come that I wil doun descende.
But nathelees, considereth this,' quod he,
'Ther nis no werkman, whatsoevere he be,   620
That may bothe werke wel and hastily;
This wol be doon at leyser parfitly.
It is no fors how longe that we pleye;
In trewe wedlok coupled be we tweye;
And blessed be the yok that we been inne,   625
For in oure actes we mowe do no sinne.
A man may do no sinne with his wyf,
Ne hurte himselven with his owene knyf;
For we han leve to pleye us by the lawe.'
Thus laboureth he til that the day gan dawe;   630
And thanne he taketh a sop in fyn clarree,
And upright in his bed thanne sitteth he,
And after that he sang ful loude and cleere,
And kiste his wif, and made wantown cheere.
He was al coltissh, ful of ragerye,   635
And ful of jargon as a flekked pye.
The slakke skin aboute his nekke shaketh.
Whil that he sang, so chaunteth he and craketh.

In many medieval romances, as in modern novels, the strongest passion is represented as being before or outside marriage, sometimes adulterous; the man suffers terribly for a lady to whom he cannot reveal his love. He must do great deeds to win her. She may, perhaps take 'pitee' on his love from her 'gentilesse'. In the medieval tales this love can be elevated to great heights of self-sacrifice and courage. Here Chaucer introduces a note of bathos: the greatest height Damyan can reach is to borrow a pen, and write a song.

- May has not yet spoken in the story which has concentrated entirely on January's feelings, though the Merchant tells us that she doesn't does give a bean for his sexual activity. Discuss with a partner how much sympathy you feel for May at this point. How much have we learnt so far about her thoughts and motivation?
- In lines 657-62 the Merchant addresses his own character, Damyan, in an apostrophe, which asks him a rhetorical question. What effect do you think Chaucer intends here?

645	**prime** nine o clock in the morning	660	**wo** suffering
649	**as usage is of wives** as is customary for wives	661	**she wol thy wo biwreye** she will betray your love
652	**no lives creature** no living creature	664	**brenneth** burns
653	**fissh, or brid, or beest, or man** [Notice again the comparison with animals.]	665	**in aventure** at risk
		667	**penner** writing case with pen and ink
657	**sely** foolish, simple	669	**compleynt or a lay** poetic lament or song
659	**shaltow** shall you	671	**heng** which hung
	fresshe blooming, lovely [Notice how frequently this adjective is applied to May, its use becoming increasingly ironic.]		

'... prively a penner gan he borwe,
And in a lettre wroot he al his sorwe'

The Merchant tells the reader that May did not think much of January's love-making, and that she stayed secluded for the next four days. He then calls Damyan foolish for loving May now that she is married. Damyan writes her a love letter, which he keeps in a silk purse over his heart.

But God woot what that May thoughte in hir herte,
Whan she him saugh up sittinge in his sherte,   640
In his night-cappe, and with his nekke lene;
She preyseth nat his pleying worth a bene.
Thanne seide he thus, 'My reste wol I take;
Now day is come, I may no lenger wake.'
And doun he leyde his heed, and sleep til prime.   645
And afterward, whan that he saugh his time,
Up riseth Januarie; but fresshe May
Heeld hire chambre unto the fourthe day,
As usage is of wives for the beste.
For every labour somtime moot han reste,   650
Or elles longe may he nat endure;
This is to seyn, no lives creature,
Be it of fissh, or brid, or beest, or man.
     Now wol I speke of woful Damyan,
That langwissheth for love, as ye shul heere;   655
Therfore I speke to him in this manere:
I seye, 'O sely Damyan, allas,
Andswere to my demaunde, as in this cas.
How shaltow to thy lady, fresshe May,
Telle thy wo? She wole alwey seye nay.   660
Eek if thou speke, she wol thy wo biwreye.
God be thyn helpe, I kan no bettre seye.'
     This sike Damyan in Venus fyr
So brenneth that he dieth for desir,
For which he putte his lyf in aventure.   665
No lenger mighte he in this wise endure,
But prively a penner gan he borwe,
And in a lettre wroot he al his sorwe,
In manere of a compleynt or a lay,
Unto his faire, fresshe lady May;   670
And in a purs of silk, heng on his sherte
He hath it put, and leyde it at his herte.

- The words 'gentil' and 'gentillesse' are used four times in 17 lines. It means both nobility of family, well-born, and noble in character. Chaucer is drawing the reader's attention to the potential irony here by repetition. One of the main points made by the Loathly Lady in the Wife of Bath's Tale is that no man can be called noble if he does not behave nobly: 'He is gentil that dooth gentil deedes'. Do you think that it is possible to inherit nobility of character? As the Tale progresses decide for yourself whether it is an appropriate term when applied to these characters.

675   **two of Tawr, was into Cancre gliden** (the moon) was in the second house of Taurus and has now moved into Cancer [Chaucer was very knowledgeable about astronomy, and his calculations show that the wedding took place at a conjunction of the planets Mars and Venus – an indication of warring and contradictory factors.]

677   **custume** custom

678   **eten in the halle** eat in the hall [in public]

679-80   **thre dayes atte leeste, Ypassed been** at least three days have passed

681   **fourthe day compleet** [May stays in her room the full four days, which was the traditional time that a noble lady would stay secluded after her wedding night.]

684   **As fressh as is the brighte someres day** as lovely as a summer's day

685   **Remembred him** he remembered [January is a conscientious householder.]

688   **entendeth nat to me?** does not attend on me

689   **ay** still

692   **letted him to doon his bisynesse** prevented him doing his job

693   **tarye** delay

694   **That me forthinketh** that grieves me

695   **gentil** noble [Does January show himself to be a good judge of character?]

696   **deyde** died

      routhe a shame, a pity

699   **therto manly and eek servisable** [Is this ironic? How manly is Damyan? And in what sense is he going to be 'servisable'?]

702   **after mete** after dinner

May stays in her chamber for the full time allowed by convention before she joins January in the hall for a feast. January realises that Damyan is missing and wonders if he is still ill. He decides to visit him.

The moone, that at noon was thilke day
That Januarie hath wedded fresshe May
In two of Tawr, was into Cancre gliden;   675
So longe hath Mayus in hir chambre abiden,
As custume is unto thise nobles alle.
A bride shal nat eten in the halle
Til dayes foure, or thre dayes atte leeste,
Ypassed been; thanne lat hire go to feeste.   680
The fourthe day compleet fro noon to noon,
Whan that the heighe masse was ydoon,
In halle sit this Januarie and May,
As fressh as is the brighte someres day.
And so bifel how that this goode man   685
Remembred him upon this Damyan,
And seyde, 'Seynte Marie, how may this be,
That Damyan entendeth nat to me?
Is he ay sik, or how may this bitide?'
His squieres, whiche that stooden ther biside,   690
Excused him by cause of his siknesse,
Which letted him to doon his bisynesse;
Noon oother cause mighte make him tarye.
'That me forthinketh,' quod this Januarie,
'He is a gentil squier, by my trouthe;   695
If that he deyde, it were harm and routhe.
He is as wys, discreet, and as secree
As any man I woot of his degree,
And therto manly, and eek servisable,
And for to been a thrifty man right able.   700
But after mete, as soone as evere I may,
I wol myself visite him, and eek May,
To doon him al the confort that I kan.'

- Read aloud lines 720-33 two or three times. What impression do you gain from Chaucer's use of words and the rhythm of the lines?
- What options does May have on being presented so dramatically with a secret letter? Do we learn anything about her from her manner of accepting it?

704 **him blessed every man** every man blessed him [However, notice that he himself doesn't visit Damyan immediately.]

712 **Dooth him disport** entertain him

714 **Have I no thing but rested me a lite** after I have had a short rest

715 **spede yow faste, for I wol abide** hurry back because I will wait

718 **marchal of his halle** master of ceremonies

720 **streight hir wey yholde** went straight away

724 **whan that his time he say** when he saw the right moment

725 **In secree wise his purs and eek his bille** secretly his purse and also his letter

726 **wille** desires

727 **withouten moore** without any explanation

728 **Save that he siketh wonder depe and soore** except that he sighed very deeply and sorrowfully

730 **discovere** betray

731 **deed** dead

kid known [He does not seem inspired to great feats of courage by his love for May.]

733 **ye gete namoore of me** [The Merchant does not comment on Damyan's actions.]

January sends May and her women to visit Damyan to cheer him up in his illness. Damyan takes the opportunity of secretly giving May the purse containing his letter. May takes the purse and hides it.

And for that word him blessed every man,
That of his bountee and his gentillesse   705
He wolde so conforten in siknesse
His squier, for it was a gentil dede.
'Dame,' quod this Januarie, 'taak good hede,
At after-mete ye with youre wommen alle,
Whan ye han been in chambre out of this halle,   710
That alle ye go se this Damyan.
Dooth him disport—he is a gentil man;
And telleth him that I wol him visite,
Have I no thing but rested me a lite;
And spede yow faste, for I wole abide   715
Til that ye slepe faste by my side.'
And with that word he gan to him to calle
A squier, that was marchal of his halle,
And tolde him certeyn thinges, what he wolde.
    This fresshe May hath streight hir wey yholde,   720
With alle hir wommen, unto Damyan.
Doun by his beddes side sit she than,
Confortinge him as goodly as she may.
This Damyan, whan that his time he say,
In secree wise his purs and eek his bille,   725
In which that he ywriten hadde his wille,
Hath put into hire hand, withouten moore,
Save that he siketh wonder depe and soore,
And softely to hire right thus seyde he:
'Mercy, and that ye nat discovere me,   730
For I am deed if that this thing be kid.'
This purs hath she inwith hir bosom hid,
And wente hire wey; ye gete namoore of me.

- Chaucer allows the Merchant to withdraw a little from the detail of the story, lines 750-5, and leave January's actions to the imagination of the reader. Do you think that this is more or less effective than an explicit description? Chaucer frequently chooses to assume a coy manner when he wishes to suggest that something rather crude is taking place.
- Chaucer mentions Venus, a Roman goddess, in line 759, and 'alle thing hath time ...' in line 760, which is a reference to Ecclesiastes chapter 3. What is the effect of this mixture of pagan and Christian references?
- Notice that in lines 736 and 746-55 May appears as the passive recipient of January's caresses.

737	**that anon** immediately	749	**be hire lief or looth** whether she wished to or not
738	**She feyned ... moot neede** she pretended that she needed to go where everyone needs to go [i.e. to the lavatory. A medieval privy would have nothing in common with a modern toilet. They were usually built into the outside wall with a wooden seat over a short vertical shaft dropping the waste into the moat or a pit.]	750	**precious** prudish **wrooth** angry
		751	**How that he wroghte** what he did
		753-4	**But heere I lete ... til evensong rong** but here I allow them to behave as they wished until the bell rang for evensong
741	**rente it al to cloutes** tore it to shreds **softly** gently [Destroying the evidence in this way rather conflicts with the romantic idea of a 'love-letter'.]	755-9	**Were it by ... Venus werkes** whether it was destiny or fortune, influences, natural causes or the position of the planets, it was a propitious time to start a love affair
		762	**grete** great
743	**studieth** thinks carefully	764	**He deme of al** may He judge all
748	**dide him encombraunce** got in his way		

64

May returns to January's bed immediately. When he is asleep she goes to the privy, reads Damyan's note, tears it up, and throws it into the toilet. She goes back to bed with January, and when he wakes he makes her remove all her clothing. The Merchant says he dare not tell what they did, or what she thought of it.

But unto Januarie ycomen is she,
That on his beddes side sit ful softe.   735
He taketh hire, and kisseth hire ful ofte,
And leyde him doun to slepe, and that anon.
She feyned hire as that she moste gon
Ther as ye woot that every wight moot neede;
And whan she of this bille hath taken heede,   740
She rente it al to cloutes atte laste,
And in the privee softely it caste.
   Who studieth now but faire fresshe May?
Adoun by olde Januarie she lay,
That sleep til that the coughe hath him awaked.   745
Anon he preyde hire strepen hire al naked;
He wolde of hire, he seyde, han som plesaunce,
And seyde hir clothes dide him encombraunce,
And she obeyeth, be hire lief or looth.
But lest that precious folk be with me wrooth,   750
How that he wroghte, I dar nat to yow telle;
Or wheither hire thoughte it paradis or helle,
But heere I lete hem werken in hir wise
Til evensong rong, and that they moste arise.
   Were it by destinee or aventure,   755
Were it by influence or by nature,
Or constellacion, that in swich estaat
The hevene stood, that time fortunaat
Was for to putte a bille of Venus werkes—
For alle thing hath time, as seyn thise clerkes—   760
To any womman, for to gete hire love,
I kan nat seye; but grete God above,
That knoweth that noon act is causelees,
He deme of al, for I wole holde my pees.

- Read the facing page through aloud two or three times and note Chaucer's use of irony. His narrator seems to suggest that May is generous, noble and kind for taking pity on Damyan's suffering. What do you think? Justify your opinions by noting down specific words and phrases.
- Write the letter which you think May might have thrust under Damyan's pillow, taking care to adopt the tone appropriate to anything you have learnt so far about her character.

766   **impression** [January wanted May to be like wax, line 218, now she has taken the 'impression' of Damyan.]

771   **I rekke noght** I don't care

774   **pitee renneth soone in gentil herte** a kind heart is easily moved to pity [This is one of Chaucer's favourite lines, here used with irony.]

775   **how excellent franchise ... avise** what noble generosity is in women, when they consider carefully

777-82   **Som tyrant is ... an homicide** some cruel women, and there are several with hearts as hard as stone, would have let him die on the spot rather than have granted him pity, and taken pleasure in their heartless pride and not cared about being a murderer

785   **verray grace** agreement to his desires [This is the language of courtly love, which echoes the grace bestowed by God. This is lacking here since what is planned is a sordid liaison. See page 107 for more information on courtly love.]

787   **unto his lust suffise** satisfy his desires

791   **sotilly** craftily

793-4   **harde him twist So secrely that no wight of it wiste** she wrung his hand, so secretly that no one knew of it

795   **and bad him been al hool** told him to recover completely

'This gentil May, fulfilled of pitee,
Right of hire hand a lettre made she'

May decides that she will take pity on Damyan and accede to his desires. She writes a letter that tells him she will sleep with him as soon as possible. She visits him and puts the letter under his pillow and tells him to get well. She then returns to January.

But sooth is this, how that this fresshe May 765
Hath take swich impression that day
Of pitee of this sike Damyan,
That from hire herte she ne drive kan
The remembrance for to doon him ese.
'Certeyn,' thoghte she, 'whom that this thing displese, 770
I rekke noght, for heere I him assure
To love him best of any creature,
Though he namoore hadde than his sherte.'
Lo, pitee renneth soone in gentil herte.
    Heere may ye se how excellent franchise 775
In wommen is, whan they hem narwe avise.
Som tyrant is, as ther by many oon,
That hath an herte as hard as any stoon,
Which wolde han lat him sterven in the place
Wel rather than han graunted him hire grace; 780
And hem rejoysen in hire crueel pride,
And rekke nat to been an homicide.
    This gentil May, fulfilled of pitee,
Right of hire hand a lettre made she,
In which she graunteth him hire verray grace. 785
Ther lakketh noght, oonly but day and place,
Wher that she mighte unto his lust suffise;
For it shal be right as he wole devise.
And whan she saugh hir time, upon a day,
To visite this Damyan gooth May, 790
And sotilly this lettre doun she threste
Under his pilwe, rede it if him leste.
She taketh him by the hand, and harde him twiste
So secrely that no wight of it wiste,
And bad him been al hool, and forth she wente 795
To Januarie, whan that he for hire sente.

Epicurus is probably the scholar referred to in line 809. His philosophy was popularly interpreted to mean that pleasure is the supreme good and main goal in life.

Priapus is mentioned in line 822 in his role as god of gardens, but it would be common knowledge to Chaucer's audience that he was also the god of sexual potency.

- Look again at lines 797-802. What do they suggest about the contents of May's letter? Do you feel pleased for Damyan? Or is there any aspect of the situation that makes you feel less sympathetic towards him?
- January's garden is described as perfect. Everything he possesses has been described by the Merchant as superlatively beautiful – even his wife. How far would you say that Chaucer is asking us to contrast the perfection of the outward appearances with the reality?

799 **He kembeth him, he preyneth him and piketh** he combs his hair, makes himself neat and adorns himself [By convention, he makes an instant recovery once the lady has agreed to his wishes.]

801-2 **he gooth as lowe As evere dide a dogge for the bowe** he bows as low as a dog trained to hunt with an archer [Again Chaucer makes a telling comparison with an animal.]

804 **For craft is al, whoso that do it kan** for guile is everything, those who can employ it do

805 **speke him good** speak highly of him

812 **honest wise** a respectable manner

813 **Shoop him to live ful deliciously** planned to live in a sensual and extravagant manner

814-5 **His housinge ... maked as a kinges** his household and his furnishings were suited to his status, made like a king's

818 **So fair a gardyn woot I nowher noon** I don't know of a more beautiful garden anywhere [For more information on the image of the garden within the Tale see page 107.]

820 **he that wroot the Romance of the Rose** [The authors of the *Roman de la Rose* were Guillaume de Loris and Jean de Meun. Chaucer had translated some of it into English. For more information see page 107.]

822-5 **Ne Priapus ne ... alwey grene** nor could Priapus, even though he is the god of gardens, describe the beauty of the garden, and the well that stood under the evergreen laurel tree [We are reminded of January's image of himself as a laurel, line 254.]

826-7 [For more information on the legend of Pluto and Proserpina see page 109.]

Damyan is immediately cured. He gets up early next morning and dresses carefully to impress May. He bows low to January. Returning to the main thread of his narrative, the Merchant tells of the luxury of January's life – he lives like a king. Now he creates a perfect walled garden.

Up riseth Damyan the nexte morwe;
Al passed was his siknesse and his sorwe.
He kembeth him, he preyneth him and piketh,
He dooth al that his lady lust and liketh;   800
And eek to Januarie he gooth as lowe
As evere dide a dogge for the bowe.
He is so plesant unto every man
(For craft is al, whoso that do it kan)
That every wight is fain to speke him good;   805
And fully in his lady grace he stood.
Thus lete I Damyan aboute his nede,
And in my tale forth I wol procede.
Somme clerkes holden that felicitee
Stant in delit, and therfore certeyn he,   810
This noble Januarie, with al his might,
In honest wise, as longeth to a knight,
Shoop him to live ful deliciously.
His housinge, his array, as honestly
To his degree was maked as a kinges.   815
Amonges othere of his honeste thinges,
He made a gardyn, walled al with stoon;
So fair a gardyn woot I nowher noon.
For, out of doute, I verraily suppose
That he that wroot the Romance of the Rose   820
Ne koude of it the beautee wel devise;
Ne Priapus ne mighte nat suffise,
Though he be god of gardyns, for to telle
The beautee of the gardyn and the welle,
That stood under a laurer alwey grene.   825
Ful ofte time he Pluto and his queene,
Proserpina, and al hire faierye,
Disporten hem and maken melodye
Aboute that welle, and daunced, as men tolde.

The rhyme of wicket/clicket (gate/key) is very powerful. It is onomatopoeic – it echoes the sound of locking or unlocking the gate of the garden. There is also the sexual imagery of the key and keyhole. At the moment only January holds the key.

- Imagine that you are speaking to a large audience and read aloud lines 845-56. Try to capture the rhetorical power of the apostrophe. Or in groups of four (narrator, January, May and Damyan) prepare a mimed scene of a significant moment which illustrates the point of the narrator's words.
- The beautiful summer garden seems the perfect setting for love and romance, and 'fresshe' May seems the ideal heroine. What aspects of January's person and his behaviour have been accentuated by Chaucer throughout the Tale, to suggest his incongruity as her partner in love?

830 **Januarie the olde** [Immediately after reminding the reader of the image of the evergreen laurel, Chaucer points out that January is, in fact, old.]

831 **Swich deyntee** took such pleasure

832 **wol no wight suffren bere** would let no one else carry

835 **whan that him leste, he it unshette** when he wished to, he unlocked it

836 **wolde paye his wyf hir dette** make love to his wife

837 **somer** summer

839 **abedde** in bed

840 **spedde** successfully

843 **dure** last, endure

845 **hap** chance

846 **scorpion** [The scorpion was the symbol of treachery.]

847 **heed** head [often 'tongue' when used as an image of person]

849 **O brotil joye, o sweete venym queynte** Oh unstable joy! Oh sweet deceiving poison! [Notice that Chaucer has used 'brotil' earlier, line 67. We have been warned.]

850 **subtilly kanst peynte** craftily can disguise

851 **yiftes** gifts

hewe of stidefastnesse the disguise of constancy

855-6 **thou has biraft him ... he to dien** you have stolen both his eyes from him, so that, grief-stricken, he wishes to die

858 **lust** pleasures

859 **Is woxen blind, and that al sodeynly** is suddenly struck blind

'He made a gardyn, walled al with stoon;
So fair a gardyn woot I nowher noon'

January wanted to retain the use of his garden entirely for himself and May. He always carried the key to the garden gate with him. He liked to make love to May in the garden in summertime. The Merchant tells us that men may not always have good fortune and January is suddenly struck blind.

This noble knight, this Januarie the olde,   830
Swich deyntee hath in it to walke and pleye,
That he wol no wight suffren bere the keye
Save he himself; for of the smale wiket
He baar alwey of silver a cliket,
With which, whan that him leste, he it unshette.   835
And whan he wolde paye his wyf hir dette
In somer seson, thider wolde he go,
And May his wyf, and no wight but they two;
And thinges whiche that were nat doon abedde,
He in the gardyn parfourned hem and spedde.   840
And in this wise, many a murye day,
Lived this Januarie and fresshe May.
But worldly joye may nat alwey dure
To Januarie, ne to no creature.
    O sodeyn hap, o thou Fortune unstable!   845
Lyk to the scorpion so deceyvable,
That flaterest with thyn heed whan thou wolt stinge;
Thy tail is deeth, thurgh thyn envenyminge.
O brotil joye, o sweete venym queynte!
O monstre, that so subtilly kanst peynte   850
Thy yiftes under hewe of stidefastnesse,
That thou deceyvest bothe moore and lesse.
Why hastow Januarie thus deceyved.
That haddest him for thy fulle freend receyved?
And now thou hast biraft him bothe his yen,   855
For sorwe of which desireth he to dien.
    Allas, this noble Januarie free,
Amidde his lust and his prosperitee,
Is woxen blind, and that al sodeynly.

After remaining entirely passive under January's hands, May is now as desperately passionate as he. But not for him.

• January is struck blind – but how effectively has he 'seen' anything, even with his physical sight intact? How does his blindness affect his behaviour towards May? Does his lack of sight open up an inner awareness?

• Notice how January is determined to hang on to his ownership of May. What do you feel about his wish that May should remain faithful to him even after his death?

862 **folye** foolishness, sin

863 **brente** burned

868 **Soul as the turtle that lost hath hire make** alone as the turtle-dove who has lost her mate [The dove was a traditional image of fidelity. The image also echoes the Song of Solomon.]

870 **His sorwe gan aswage** his grief began to diminish

871 **it may noon oother be** the situation could not be any different

873-4 **he may nat ... in oon** except that he could not refrain from being consumed by jealousy

875 **outrageous** excessive

876-8 **That neither ... or go** [Chaucer frequently uses a triple negative (see page 10) for emphasis. Look how he piles up the negatives here to create the sense of January's panic.]

879 **But if that he had hond on hire alway** unless he always had his hand on her

881 **beningnely** graciously

882 **she moot oother dien sodeynly** she must either die immediately

883 **han him as hir leste** have him as she desires

884 **waiteth** expects (the time)

889 **purpos** intentions

January's worst anguish concerns May. He is jealous. He doesn't want her to be lover or wife to any other man ever. He wants her to mourn his death as a widow for the rest of her life. Gradually his grief eases but he won't let May go beyond his touch. She and Damyan bemoan the fact that they cannot have sex.

He wepeth and he waileth pitously;   860
And therwithal the fyr of jalousie,
Lest that his wyf sholde falle in som folye,
So brente his herte that he wolde fain
That som man bothe hire and him had slain.
For neither after his deeth, nor in his lyf,   865
Ne wolde he that she were love ne wyf,
But evere live as widwe in clothes blake,
Soul as the turtle that lost hath hire make.
But atte laste, after a month or tweye,
His sorwe gan aswage, sooth to seye;   870
For whan he wiste it may noon oother be,
He paciently took his adversitee,
Save, out of doute, he may nat forgoon
That he nas jalous everemoore in oon;
Which jalousye it was so outrageous,   875
That neither in halle, n'in noon oother hous,
Ne in noon oother place, neverthemo,
He nolde suffre hire for to ride or go,
But if that he had hond on hire alway;
For which ful ofte wepeth fresshe May,   880
That loveth Damyan so beningnely
That she moot outher dien sodeynly,
Or elles she moot han him as hir leste.
She waiteth whan hir herte wolde breste.
    Upon that oother side Damyan   885
Bicomen is the sorwefulleste man
That evere was; for neither night ne day
Ne mighte he speke a word to fresshe May,
As to his purpos, of no swich mateere,
But if that Januarie moste it heere,   890
That hadde an hand upon hire everemo.

Juno asked Argus with his hundred eyes to guard Io when she suspected that her husband, Zeus, was having a love affair with her. Zeus managed to outwit him. However, in traditional stories Argus was easily tricked by clever women.

- May takes an impression of the key in warm wax. This reminds the reader of January's wish to mould her like wax himself, line 218. What point do you think that Chaucer is making?
- Chaucer quotes Ovid's grand statement (line 915) that 'love will always find a way'; but are we really talking of 'love' at any point in this tale? Do you think that Chaucer intended to suggest that May and Damyan are in love? If you think that he didn't, what point is he making?

892-4 **But nathelees ... his entente** but nevertheless, by writing letters, and secret signs, he knew what she meant, and she also knew the aim of his intentions

895-6 **O Januarie ... saille** O January, what good would it do you to see as far as the horizon? [This is another apostrophe, this time to blind January.]

897-8 **For as good ... man may se** you may as well be deceived when you are blind as when you can see [Perhaps lines 897-8 contain one of the major lessons of the Tale: when January could physically see, he was morally blind.]

899 **Argus** [Argus was a 100-eyed giant in classical mythology.]

900 **poure, pryen** both words mean to gaze intently

901-2 **Yet was he blent ... be nat so** yet he was blinded and, God knows, so are many more who are certain it cannot be so

903 **Passe over is an ese** what you don't know won't hurt you [*literally:* to overlook gives ease]

909 **The cliket countrefeted prively** secretly copied the key

913-5 **O noble Ovide ... manere?** Oh noble Ovid, you told the truth, God knows, when you said that love will always find a way, no matter how long or difficult

916-9 **By Piramus ... swich a sleighte** this can be learned from the story of Pyramus and Thisbe – though they were kept strictly apart, they eventually arranged to elope by whispering through a wall, a device that no one discovered [*Metamorphoses*, Ovid's original story is tragic, though Shakespeare transformed it into a comedy in *A Midsummer Night's Dream*.]

May and Damyan communicate by signs. May manages to make a wax impression of the key to the gate of the garden. Damyan has a key made. The Merchant comments that love will find a way.

But natheless, by writing to and fro,
And privee signes, wiste he what she mente,
And she knew eek the fin of his entente.
   O Januarie, what mighte it thee availle,   895
Thogh thou mighte se as fer as shippes saille?
For as good is blind deceyved be
As to be deceyved whan a man may se.
   Lo, Argus, which that hadde an hondred yen,
For al that evere he koude poure or pryen,   900
Yet was he blent, and, God woot, so been mo,
That wenen wisly that it be nat so.
Passe over is an ese, I sey namoore.
   This fresshe May, that I spak of so yoore,
In warm wex hath emprented the cliket   905
That Januarie bar of the smale wiket,
By which into his gardyn ofte he wente,
And Damyan, that knew al hire entente,
The cliket countrefeted prively.
Ther nis namoore to seye, but hastily   910
Som wonder by this cliket shal bitide,
Which ye shul heeren, if ye wole abide.
   O noble Ovide, ful sooth seystou, God woot,
What sleighte is it, thogh it be long and hoot,
That Love nil finde it out in som manere?   915
By Piramus and Tesbee may men leere;
Thogh they were kept ful longe streite overal,
They been accorded, rowninge thurgh a wal,
Ther no wight koude han founde out swich a sleighte.

- Lines 925-36 are a paraphrase of the Song of Solomon 2.10-14, 4.7-12. (My beloved spoke, and said to me, Rise, my love, my fair one, and come away. For lo, the winter is past, the rain is over and gone. The flowers appear on the earth; the time of the singing of birds is come, and the voice of the turtle is heard in our land. 2.10-12.) The Merchant uses the word 'lewed' to describe this beautiful love poetry. In Chaucer's time 'lewed' had more than one meaning; obscene, but also unlearned or ignorant. Do you think that a) Chaucer thinks that the words are obscene and ignorant? b) the Merchant thinks that the words are obscene and ignorant? c) January is corrupting their meaning by using them to tempt May to 'disport' in the garden?
- Is May worthy of the poetic praise as she signs to her lover to go first into the garden? You could look back through the Tale and notice how Chaucer has conveyed the ironic contrast between fantasy and reality through his use of language. He increasingly uses abstract courtly vocabulary ('gentilesse', 'noble knyght', 'fresshe May' and so on), and opposes it with comparisons with animals, coarse physical descriptions and uncouth behaviour.

920-1	**er that dayes ... month of Juin** on or before the 8th of June	928	**reynes weete** wet rain
		929	**columbin** dove-like
923	**Thurgh egging of his wyf** with the encouragement of his wife [Why does she 'egg him on'?]	934	**No spot of thee ne knew I al my lyf** I know of no sin in you all my life
924	**no wight but they tweye** just the two of them	939	**biforn with his cliket** go in before them using his key
927	**The turtles vois is herd** the voice of the turtle-dove is heard	941	**stirte** rushed
		942	**no wight mighte it se neither yheere** no-one saw or heard

During June, May urges January to visit the garden, and he uses the words of the Song of Solomon
to invite her to go with him. She makes signs to Damyan that he should go first and conceal
himself.

But now to purpos: er that dayes eighte   920
Were passed, er the month of Juin, bifil
That Januarie hath caught so greet a wil,
Thurgh egging of his wyf, him for to pleye
In his gardyn, and no wight but they tweye,
That in a morwe unto his May seith he: 925
'Ris up, my wyf, my love, my lady free,
The turtles vois is herd, my dowve sweete;
The winter is goon with alle his reynes weete.
Com forth now, with thine eyen columbin,
How fairer been thy brestes than is wyn.   930
The gardyn is enclosed al aboute;
Com forth, my white spouse, out of doute
Thou hast me wounded in myn herte, O wyf,
No spot of thee ne knew I al my lyf.
Com forth, and lat us taken oure disport;   935
I chees thee for my wyf and my confort.'
    Swiche olde lewed wordes used he.
On Damyan a signe made she,
That he sholde go biforn with his cliket.
This Damyan thanne hath opened the wiket,   940
And in he stirte, and that in swich manere
That no wight mighte it se neither yheere,
And stille he sit under a bussh anon.

- Comment on January's desire to give May everything he possesses at this comparatively late stage in their marriage.
- In what ways do you think that Chaucer increases the reader's sympathy for January here, and for what purpose?
- Chaucer uses the rhyme of 'knyf' and 'wyf' in lines 951-2 for the second time in the Tale. Look back at lines 627-8 and consider the effect of the repetition.

947 **clapt to the wiket sodeynly** shut the gate sharply

951-2 **Levere ich hadde to dien on a knyf, Than thee offende** I had rather be stabbed to death than to displease you

953 **chees** chose

954 **Noght for** not by any means for
coveitise greed
doutelees without a doubt

957 **Beth to me trewe** be faithful to me

961 **chartres** contracts, deeds

962 **er sonne reste** before sundown

963 **wisly** certainly

964 **in covenant ye me kisse** kiss me to seal the bargain

965 **wite me noght** do not blame me

968 **unlikly** unsuitable

970 **forbere** endure

971 **verray** true

*'This Januarie, as blind as is a stoon,
With Mayus in his hand, and no wight mo,
Into his fresshe gardyn is ago'*

78

Blind January takes May by the hand and leads her into the garden where he declares his love for her. He promises that the next day he will give her everything he possesses because he loves her so much. He asks her not to be offended by his jealousy because he cannot bear to be out of her company.

This Januarie, as blind as is a stoon,
With Mayus in his hand, and no wight mo,   945
Into his fresshe gardyn is ago,
And clapte to the wiket sodeynly,
  'Now wyf,' quod he, 'heere nis but thou and I,
That art the creature that I best love.
For by that Lord that sit in hevene above,   950
Levere ich hadde to dien on a knyf,
Than thee offende, trewe deere wyf!
For Goddes sake, thenk how I thee chees,
Noght for no coveitise, doutelees,
But oonly for the love I had to thee.   955
And though that I be oold, and may nat see,
Beth to me trewe, and I wol telle yow why.
Thre thinges, certes, shal ye winne therby:
First, love of Crist, and to youreself honour,
And al myn heritage, toun and tour;   960
I yeve it yow, maketh chartres as yow leste;
This shal be doon to-morwe er sonne reste,
So wisly God my soule bringe in blisse.
I prey yow first, in covenant ye me kisse;
And though that I be jalous, wite me noght.   965
Ye been so depe enprented in my thoght
That, whan that I considere youre beautee,
And therwithal the unlikly elde of me,
I may nat, certes, though I sholde die,
Forbere to been out of youre compaignye   970
For verray love; this is withouten doute.
Now kis me, wyf, and lat us rome aboute.'

- Lines 976-94 are the first words assigned to May in the Tale. She replies to the reasons why January says she should be faithful to him; she refers to her spiritual well-being, and her honour, though not to his gifts. She claims that it is men's infidelity that makes them suspect women. What impression of her character do you think Chaucer is suggesting here?
- The situation on the previous page and this one has been set up to allow us, the audience, to appreciate the ironic complexity of what we see. Using the facts at your disposal, compose a short piece of writing for January and another for May in which the inner thoughts, hopes and fears of each character are revealed. At this stage in the Tale who seems most to blame – January or May?

975   **first and forward** first of all

978-80 **of my wifhod ... my body bond**
[May refers January to their marriage vows – she promised to be faithful to him when she was bound to him by the priest. There is perhaps an ironic reference to the fact that he always has his hand on her and that she is more literally than figuratively 'bound' to him.]

983-9 **By the leve ... do me drenche** [Her immediate response to his doubts, and her request to be put in a sack and drowned if she is ever unfaithful, might strike the reader as somewhat exaggerated.]

986   **empeyre so my name** injure my reputation

992   **wommen have repreve of yow ay newe** women get nothing but reproaches from men

993   **contenance** kind of behaviour
       leeve believe

994   **repreeve** reproof, condemnation

999   **charged** laden

1000   **verraily** truly

1002   **wel bet** much better
       make mate, husband

1004   **werchen shal** should act

May promises that she will be faithful to her husband for her soul's sake. He can put her in a sack and drown her if she is ever false to him. She asks why he should doubt her when it is men who are unfaithful. She signs to Damyan to climb a tree.

This fresshe May, whan she thise wordes herde,
Beningnely to Januarie answerde,
But first and forward she bigan to wepe.   975
'I have,' quod she, 'a soule for to kepe
As wel as ye, and also myn honour,
And of my wifhod thilke tendre flour,
Which that I have assured in youre hond,
Whan that the preest to yow my body bond;   980
Wherfore I wole answere in this manere,
By the leve of yow, my lord so deere:
I prey to God that nevere dawe the day
That I ne sterve, as foule as womman may,
If evere I do unto my kin that shame,   985
Or elles I empeyre so my name,
That I be fals; and if I do that lak,
Do strepe me and put me in a sak,
And in the nexte river do me drenche.
I am a gentil womman and no wenche.   990
Why speke ye thus? But men been evere untrewe,
And wommen have repreve of yow ay newe.
Ye han noon oother contenance, I leeve,
But speke to us of untrust and repreeve.'
    And with that word she saugh wher Damyan   995
Sat in the bussh, and coughen she bigan,
And with hir finger signes made she
That Damyan sholde climbe upon a tree,
That charged was with fruit, and up he wente.
For verraily he knew al hire entente,   1000
And every signe that she koude make,
Wel bet than Januarie, hir owene make;
For in a lettre she hadde toold him al
Of this matere, how he werchen shal.
And thus I lete him sitte upon the pyrie,   1005
And Januarie and May rominge ful myrie.

It is only at line 1005 that Chaucer tells us that Damyan is sitting in a pear tree –
'pyrie'. The comic story of the pear tree was almost certainly well known to his
audience. It was a popular tale, also told in Boccaccio's *Decameron*. (See page 107.)
He then raises dramatic tension by introducing a digression, leaving his audience to
wonder what will happen to the three main protagonists. The elevated poetic
language of 1007-12 was a conventional method of marking a pause in a story.

- In lines 1007-12 the Merchant describes the beauty of the day in poetic language,
  including astrological influences. This was of great topical interest. In illuminated
  manuscripts of books of hours you will see pictorial representations of the heavens.
  Try writing a short description of the day yourself in a similar style.
- Some information about the myth of Pluto and Proserpina is on page 109. What
  variations and additions seem to you to be Chaucer's? What is the effect produced
  by choosing these particular gods for the garden?

1008	**Phebus hath of gold his stremes doun ysent** Phoebus (the sun) has sent down his gold rays	1025	**ther may no wight seye nay** no-one can deny it
1010	**He was ... in Geminis** the sun was in Gemini	1026	**preveth** proves it
1011	**declinacion** the time of least influence	1029	**brotilnesse** fickleness
1012	**exaltacion** the time of Jupiter's greatest influence	1031	**sapience** wisdom
1013	**And so bifel, that brighte morwe-tide** and so it happened, that bright morning	1033	**To every wight that wit and reson kan** to every man that has intelligence and common sense
1021	**How in his grisely carte he hire fette** How he fetched her in his terrifying carriage	1034	**bountee** virtue, excellence
		1035-6	**Amonges a thousand men ... foond I noon** I can find one (virtuous) man in a thousand, but not one in all women [Ecclesiastes Chapter 7 verse 28]

The Merchant says that he will leave Damyan up the tree and January and May to walk in the garden while he describes the beauty of the day. Pluto and Proserpina are also in the walled garden, debating the infidelity of women. Pluto says that he could find a million stories of women's deceitfulness.

   Bright was the day, and blew the firmament;
Phebus hath of gold his stremes doun ysent,
To gladen every flour with his warmnesse.
He was that time in Geminis, as I gesse,   1010
But litel fro his declinacion
Of Cancer, Jovis exaltacion.
And so bifel, that brighte morwe-tide,
That in that gardyn, in the ferther side,
Pluto, that is king of Faierye,   1015
And many a lady in his compaignye,
Folwinge his wyf, the queene Proserpina,
Which that he ravisshed out of Ethna
Whil that she gadered floures in the mede—
In Claudian ye may the stories rede,   1020
How in his grisely carte he hire fette—
This king of Fairye thanne adoun him sette
Upon a bench of turves, fressh and grene,
And right anon thus seyde he to his queene:
   'My wyf,' quod he, 'ther may no wight seye nay;   1025
Th'experience so preveth every day
The tresons whiche that wommen doon to man.
Ten hondred thousand [tales] tellen I kan
Notable of youre untrouthe and brotilnesse.
O Salomon, wys, and richest of richesse,   1030
Fulfild of sapience and of worldly glorie,
Ful worthy been thy wordes to memorie
To every wight that wit and reson kan.
Thus preiseth he yet the bountee of man:
"Amonges a thousand men yet foond I oon,   1035
But of wommen alle foond I noon."

- Pluto seems very cultured for the King of the Underworld. He quotes from the Bible (Solomon and Ecclesiasticus) and he defends the betrayed January. Pluto and Proserpina seem to see themselves as self-appointed defenders of their own sex. Write a defence of your own sex, responding to one of their arguments.
- What effect is achieved by mixing Christian and pagan ideas in this tale? (For example, in this episode there is the Garden of Eden, Solomon, and Pluto – there are other occasions, such as the marriage feast, where there also is a mixture of pagan and Christian images.)

1038	**Jhesus, *filius Syrak*** not Jesus Christ, but Jesus the author of Ecclesiasticus	1048	**have ayen his eyen sight** regain his sight
1039	**Ne speketh of yow but seelde reverence** seldom speaks of you with respect	1052	**Wol ye so?** is that what you want?
		1053	**by my moodres sires soule** by my mother's father's soul (Saturn)
1040	**corrupt pestilence** terrible infectious diseases	1054	**I shal yeven hire suffisant answere** I shall give her a suitable reply
1042	**Ne se ye nat** do you not see	1056	**in any gilt ytake** found in a guilty situation
1044	**His owene man shal make him cokewold** his own servant will cuckold him	1060-1	**Al hadde ... visage it hardily** even if a man has seen it with his own eyes, yet shall we women face it out boldly
1045	**Lo, where he sit, the lechour, in the tree** [The Merchant draws attention to the visual image of Damyan sitting in the pear tree.]	1063	**lewed as gees** silly as geese

Couple embracing in a garden (detail)

Pluto cites evidence from the Bible for the unreliability of women, and then turns to the example in front of him: Damyan sitting in the tree at the invitation of May who is preparing to deceive her old blind husband. Pluto says he will restore January's eyesight. Proserpina replies that she will bestow a suitable and convincing excuse to May, and that all women are excellent liars.

Thus seith the king that knoweth your wikkednesse.
And Jhesus, *filius Syrak*, as I gesse,
Ne speketh of yow but seelde reverence.
A wilde fyr and corrupt pestilence   1040
So falle upon youre bodies yet to-night.
Ne se ye nat this honurable knight,
By cause, allas, that he is blind and old,
His owene man shal make him cokewold.
Lo, where he sit, the lechour, in the tree.   1045
Now wol I graunten, of my magestee,
Unto this olde, blinde, worthy knight
That he shal have ayen his eyen sight,
Whan that his wyf wold doon him vileynye.
Thanne shal he knowen al hire harlotrye,   1050
Bothe in repreve of hire and othere mo.'
    'Ye shal?' quod Proserpine, 'Wol ye so?
Now by my moodres sires soule I swere
That I shal yeven hire suffisant answere,
And alle wommen after, for hir sake;   1055
That, though they be in any gilt ytake,
With face boold they shulle hemself excuse,
And bere hem doun that wolden hem accuse.
For lak of answere noon of hem shal dien.
Al hadde man seyn a thing with bothe his yen,   1060
Yit shul we wommen visage it hardily,
And wepe, and swere, and chide subtilly,
So that ye men shul been as lewed as gees.

- Here, Pluto and Proserpina argue that men and women will never understand one another. Do you think that the relationship between men and women is inevitably one of conflict? In this tale Chaucer seems to be suggesting that this is so, though elsewhere in *The Canterbury Tales* other stories take a different point of view.
- What evidence is there from the Tale that Pluto and Proserpina are more 'god-like' than ordinary men and women?

1064 **What rekketh me of youre auctoritees?** what do I care for your authorities?

1066 **of us wommen fooles many oon** found many fools among us women

1068-9 **Yet hath ther … vertuous** yet many other men found plenty of faithful, excellent, virtuous women

1072 **geestes** tales, legends

1074 **ne be nat wrooth, al be it so** do not be angry, even if it is so

1076 **sentence** sense

1077-8 **in sovereyn bontee … he ne she** in perfect goodness, there is none but God, neither man nor woman

1083 **eek** also

1084 **moore forbode is?** is more forbidden

1085-6 **Pardee … idolastre** By God, as much as you want to gloss over his reputation, he was a lecher and a worshipper of false gods [Here is the irony that a mythological goddess is criticising Solomon.]

1087 **elde** old age

verray God forsook abandoned the true God

1088 **ne hadde** had not

book Bible

1089 **Yspared him for his fadres sake** forgiven him for the sake of his father

1090 **rather than he wolde** sooner than he wanted

Proserpina becomes angry and rejects Pluto's arguments. She says some men criticise women but that there are plenty of other men who value them. She is also angry that Pluto places so much dependence on Solomon's opinions. She says Solomon's behaviour during his life makes his views worthless.

What rekketh me of youre auctoritees?
I woot wel that this Jew, this Salomon,   1065
Foond of us wommen fooles many oon.
But though that he ne foond no good womman,
Yet hath ther founde many another man
Wommen ful trewe, ful goode, and vertuous.
Witnesse on hem that dwelle in Cristes hous;   1070
With martirdom they preved hire constance.
The Romain geestes eek make remembrance
Of many a verray, trewe wyf also.
But, sire, ne be nat wrooth, al be it so,
Though that he seyde he foond no good womman,   1075
I prey yow take the sentence of the man;
He mente thus, that in sovereyn bontee
Nis noon but God, but neither he ne she.
     Ey, for verray God, that nis but oon,
What make ye so muche of Salomon?   1080
What though he made a temple, Goddes hous?
What though he were riche and glorious?
So made he eek a temple of false goddis.
How mighte he do a thing that moore forbode is?
Pardee, as faire as ye his name emplastre,   1085
He was a lecchour and an idolastre,
And in his elde he verray God forsook;
And if that God ne hadde, as seith the book,
Yspared him for his fadres sake, he sholde
Have lost his regne rather than he wolde.   1090

- Read aloud lines 1091-98, Proserpina's conclusion, and notice how Chaucer indicates the sense of her mood in the way that he uses punctuation and the sound of the words. In what ways does the inclusion of Pluto and Proserpina add an extra dimension to the story?

1091-2	**I sette right noght ... a boterflye** I don't give a butterfly for all that you write of the wickedness of women
1095-6	**For sithen ... brouke my tresses** because he said that women are mere chatterers, I won't stop criticising him as I long as I live [*literally:* as long as I keep my hair]
1100	**ooth** oath
1103	**it sit me noght to lie** it does not befit me to break my word
1107	**I wol no lenger yow contrarie** I will no longer contradict you
1110	**Singeth ful murier than the papejay** is singing more merrily than a parrot
1112	**aleyes** garden paths
1113	**againes thilke pyrie** in front of this pear tree

Proserpina continues to defend women angrily from all criticism. Pluto tells her not to be annoyed and gives in. But, he warns her, he has sworn to give January back his sight and, as he is a king, he cannot break his word. She replies that she, as queen, must also keep her word to give May a suitable response. The Merchant then turns his attention back to January and May strolling in the garden and Damyan sitting in the pear tree.

I sette right noght, of al the vileynye
That ye of wommen write, a boterflye.
I am a womman, nedes moot I speke,
Or elles swelle til myn herte breke.
For sithen he seyde that we been jangleresses,   1095
As evere hool I moote brouke my tresses,
I shal nat spare, for no curteisye,
To speke him harm that wolde us vileynye.'
   'Dame,' quod this Pluto, 'be no lenger wrooth;
I yeve it up, but sith I swoor myn ooth   1100
That I wolde graunten him his sighte ageyn,
My word shal stonde, I warne yow certeyn.
I am a king, it sit me noght to lie.'
   'And I,' quod she, 'a queene of Fayerye.
Hir answere shal she have, I undertake.   1105
Lat us namoore wordes heerof make;
For sothe, I wol no lenger yow contrarie.'
   Now lat us turne again to Januarie,
That in the gardyn with his faire May
Singeth ful murier than the papejay,   1110
'Yow love I best, and shal, and oother noon.'
So longe aboute the aleyes is he goon,
Til he was come againes thilke pyrie
Where as this Damyan sitteth ful myrie
An heigh among the fresshe leves grene.   1115

- Line 1116 is the last time that May is called 'fresshe May'. Look back at how many times she has been described as 'fresshe' which means young, blooming and lovely, and consider all the ironies Chaucer has created by the repetition. Here she is also described as bright and shining.
- Do you think that Chaucer makes January ridiculous or pathetic, as he hugs the pear tree for May to climb on his back to reach her lover? Do you have any sympathy for him?
- Does May's cleverness make you admire her? Remember that January wanted a young wife who could be manipulated as easily as warm wax. Who is the manipulator here?

1117	**sike** sigh	1135	**Mighte I yow helpen with myn herte blood** I would help you with my heart's blood
1119	**han of the peres** have one of the pears		
1123	**in my plit** in my condition [She is implying that she is pregnant.]	1137	**twiste** branch
		1138-9	**Ladies, I prey ... a rude man** ladies, don't be angry with me, I can't say this politely; I'm a plain man
1126-7	**Allas ... that I ne had heer a knave That koude climbe** I'm sorry I haven't a servant here that could climb the tree		
		1141	**throng** thrust
		1146	**Ne was ther nevere man of thing so fain** there was never a man so happy about anything
1128	**no fors** it's not important		
1130	**The pyrie inwith youre armes for to take** put your arms round the trunk of the pear tree		

May tells January that, like all women in her condition, she has sudden cravings. Hers is for a pear. He wishes there was a page to climb the tree for her, but she says she can manage if she climbs on his back. Whilst she and Damyan are engaged in sexual activity, Pluto gives January back his sight.

This fresshe May, that is so bright and sheene,
Gan for to sike, and seyde, 'Allas, my side.
Now sire,' quod she, 'for aught that may bitide,
I moste han of the peres that I see,
Or I moot die, so soore longeth me   1120
To eten of the smale peres grene.
Help, for hir love that is of hevene queene.
I telle yow wel, a womman in my plit
May han to fruit so greet an appetit
That she may dien, but she of it have.'   1125
   'Allas,' quod he, 'that I ne had heer a knave
That koude climbe. Allas, allas,' quod he,
'For I am blind.' 'Ye, sire, no fors,' quod she;
'But wolde ye vouche sauf, for Goddes sake,
The pyrie inwith youre armes for to take,   1130
For wel I woot that ye mistruste me,
Thanne sholde I climbe wel ynogh,' quod she,
'So I my foot mighte sette upon youre bak.'
   'Certes,' quod he, 'theron hal be no lak,
Mighte I yow helpen wih myn herte blood.'   1135
He stoupeth down, and on his bak she stood,
And caughte hire by a twiste, and up she gooth.
Ladies, I prey yow that ye be nat wrooth;
I kan nat glose, I am a rude man—
And sodeynly anon this Damyan   1140
Gan pullen up the smok, and in he throng.
   And whan that Pluto saugh this grete wrong,
To Januarie he gaf again his sighte,
And made him se as wel as evere he mighte.
And whan that he hadde caught his sighte again,   1145
Ne was ther nevere man of thing so fain,
But on his wif his thoght was everemo.

91

- What do you think of the 'suffisant answere' given to May by Proserpina? Do you find it convincing?
- The word 'kinde', line 1179, has two meanings: a) generous and b) of the same kind. Chaucer is being ironic here. January has married her out of lust; she has had an encounter with Damyan for the same reason.

1149-51 **Damyan ... speke uncurteisly** Damyan had treated his wife in such a way that cannot be described, unless I put it crudely

1152-3 **And up he ... child shal die** he set up such a yelling and a roaring, like a mother with a dying child

1155 **stronge lady stoore** bold, crude woman

1156 **what eyleth yow?** what's wrong with you?

1158 **I have yow holpe on bothe youre eyen blinde** I've helped you to regain your sight

1160 **as me was taught** I was told

1161 **Was no thing bet** there was nothing better

1164 **'Strugle,' quod he, 'ye algate in it wente'** 'Struggle,' he said, 'it went wholly in.'

1166 **He swived thee** he screwed you

1167 **hals** neck

1169 **if that ye mighte se** if you could truly see

1171 **Ye han som glimsing, and no parfit sighte** your sight is blurred and not perfect

1174 **me thoughte he dide thee so** I thought he was doing it to you [January is already beginning to doubt.]

1175 **ye maze** you are bewildered

1176 **This thank have I for I have maad yow see** this is all the thanks I get for restoring your sight

92

When January sees what Damyan is doing with his wife, he begins shouting. May tells him that
she was told that if she struggled with a man in a tree it would magically restore her husband's
sight. January doesn't believe her; he says he saw what was going on. She persuades him that his
newly restored sight was still blurred.

Up to the tree he caste his eyen two,
And saugh that Damyan his wyf had dressed
In swich manere it may nat been expressed,   1150
But if I wolde speke uncurteisly;
And up he yaf a roring and a cry,
As dooth the mooder whan the child shal die:
'Out, help; allas, harrow!' he gan to crye,
'O stronge lady stoore, what dostow?'   1155
   And she answerde, 'Sire, what eyleth yow?
Have pacience and resoun in youre minde!
I have yow holpe on bothe youre eyen blinde.
Up peril of my soule, I shal nat lien,
As me was taught, to heele with youre eyen,   1160
Was no thing bet, to make yow to see,
Than struggle with a man upon a tree.
God woot, I dide it in ful good entente.'
   'Strugle,' quod he, 'ye algate in it wente.
God yeve yow bothe on shames deth to dien.   1165
He swived thee, I saugh it with mine yen,
And elles be I hanged by the hals!'
   'Thanne is,' quod she, 'my medicine fals;
For certeinly, if that ye mighte se,
Ye wolde nat seyn thise wordes unto me.   1170
Ye han som glimsing, and no parfit sighte.'
   'I se,' quod he, 'as wel as evere I mighte,
Thonked be God, with bothe mine eyen two,
And by my trouthe, me thoughte he dide thee so.'
   'Ye maze, maze, goode sire,' quod she;   1175
'This thank have I for I have maad yow see.
Allas,' quod she, 'that evere I was so kinde!'

- Perhaps wisely January accepts her story. Rejecting his wife would make him look a fool (divorce was almost impossible in the Middle Ages, as it still is in the Roman Catholic Church). Do you think he has done the right thing?
- Write a short continuation of the Tale, saying what you think will be the future for the three of them.
- To what extent do you feel that Chaucer has written a story from which lessons may be learned even today? Is it sensible to choose a marriage partner on the basis of fantasy?

1179 **my lief** my dear

1180 **yvele apaid** displeased, upset

1181 **I wende han seyn** I thought I saw

1184 **ye may wene as yow lest** you may think what you like

1188 **adawed verraily** fully awake

1190 **sodeynly so wel yse** immediately see perfectly

1193 **ysatled** settled

1194 **Ther may ful many a sighte yow bigile** there may be many sights that fool you

1196 **weneth** believes

1198 **He that misconceyveth, he misdemeth** he who misunderstands, misjudges

1201 **clippeth hire ful ofte** embraces her often

1203 **And to his palays hoom he hath hire lad** and he led her home to his palace

January accepts her excuse though he still thinks he saw May and Damyan together. She convinces him it was just faulty sight and tells him to take care he doesn't misunderstand. January gladly kisses her and takes her back to his palace.

'Now, dame,' quod he, 'lat al passe out of minde.
Com doun, my lief, and if I have missaid,
God helpe me so, as I am yvele apaid.   1180
But, by my fader soule, I wende han seyn
How that this Damyan hadde by thee leyn,
And that thy smok hadde leyn upon his brest.'
   'Ye, sire,' quod she, 'ye may wene as yow lest.
But, sire, a man that waketh out of his sleep,   1185
He may nat sodeynly wel taken keep
Upon a thing, ne seen it parfitly,
Til that he be adawed verraily.
Right so a man that longe hath blind ybe,
Ne may nat sodeynly so wel yse,   1190
First whan his sighte is newe come ageyn,
As he that hath a day or two yseyn.
Til that youre sighte ysatled be a while,
Ther may ful many a sighte yow bigile.
Beth war, I prey yow; for, by hevene king,   1195
Ful many a man weneth to seen a thing,
And it is al another than it semeth.
He that misconceyveth, he misdemeth.'
And with that word she leep doun fro the tree.
   This Januarie, who is glad but he?   1200
He kisseth hire, and clippeth hire ful ofte,
And on hire wombe he stroketh hire ful softe,
And to his palays hoom he hath hire lad.
Now, goode men, I pray yow to be glad.
Thus endeth heere my tale of Januarie;
God blesse us, and his mooder Seinte Marie!   1205

Heere is ended the Marchantes Tale of Januarie.

- Read the facing page aloud with a partner two or three times and discuss how Chaucer distinguishes between the voice of the Host and the voice of the narrator of the Merchant's Tale. Do you feel that there is a difference between the tone of the Merchant's Epilogue and the Tale itself? How would you describe the difference?
- Although the Host seems to think this tale is about the perfidious nature of women, do the men in the tale seem any more admirable?
- List the faults that seem to be most commonly associated with women – then make a similar list for men, taking your ideas from this tale. What aspects of male/female relationships seem to have been entirely ignored by the Merchant? Does this suggest anything about his own character? What clues to the Merchant's character did you obtain from Chaucer's initial description of him? Do you think that Chaucer is using this man's tale and the way he tells it to make observations about the way some people behave? If so, do you feel that people behave differently today?

1207	**Ey, Goddes mercy!** Now God help us!
1208-9	**Lo, whiche sleightes and subtilitees In wommen been** look what tricks and treachery are in women
1211	**sely** innocent, naive
1212	**And from the soothe evere wol they weyve** they will always deviate from the truth
1213	**it preveth weel** it is well proven
1215	**povre** poor
1216	**but** except
	labbing shrewe gossiping hag
1219	**But wite ye what? In conseil be it seyd** but do you know what? I'll tell you in secret
1220	**Me reweth soore I am unto hire teyd** I bitterly repent that I am tied to her
1221	**rekenen** enumerate
1222	**to nice** too foolish
1224	**of somme of this meynee** by someone from this company [The implication is that he means the Wife of Bath.]
1225	**of** by
1226	**Sin wommen konnen outen swich chaffare** since women know how to display such matters
1227	**eek my wit suffiseth nat therto, To tellen al** also my wits are not up to telling everything

The Host is shocked by the Tale and says all women are industrious in deceiving men. He believes his own wife is faithful, but she nags and has plenty of other faults as well, and he regrets being tied to her. He says he won't describe her faults in detail in case one of the women in the company of pilgrims tells his wife when they get back.

'Ey, Goddes mercy!' seyde oure Hooste tho,
'Now swich a wyf I pray God kepe me fro!
Lo, whiche sleightes and subtilitees
In wommen been. For ay as bisy as bees   1210
Been they, us sely men for to deceyve,
And from the soothe evere wol they weyve;
By this Marchauntes tale it preveth weel.
But doutelees, as trewe as any steel
I have a wyf, though that she povre be,   1215
But of hir tonge, a labbing shrewe is she,
And yet she hath an heep of vices mo;
Therof no fors, lat alle swiche thinges go.
But wite ye what? In conseil be it seyd,
Me reweth soore I am unto hire teyd.   1220
For, and I sholde rekenen every vice
Which that she hath, ywis I were to nice;
And cause why, it sholde reported be
And toold to hire of somme of this meynee,—
Of whom, it nedeth nat for to declare,   1225
Sin wommen konnen outen swich chaffare;
And eek my wit suffiseth nat therto,
To tellen al, wherfore my tale is do.'

Looking back at the Merchant's Tale

It is possible to divide the Merchant's Tale into sections and this can enable the reader to begin to analyse the way that Chaucer has structured it.

Lines 33-186 This is where the Merchant praises marriage and January becomes progressively more committed to his particular ideas about wedlock. It is a way to avoid the sin of fornication, which he admits he has always committed, 'for wedlok is so esy and so clene'. Though he speaks of the spiritual justification for marriage there is a much greater concentration on the material convenience and pleasure to be obtained from an obedient wife. His praise of marriage becomes increasingly unrealistic and therefore almost savagely sarcastic when contrasted with the Merchant's thorough disenchantment after only two months' experience.

Lines 187-256 January calls his friends to tell them of his decision. He acknowledges his own age but he compares himself to a blossoming tree or an evergreen. This wilful self-delusion prefigures the disillusion which occurs, appropriately enough, in a garden. He describes the kind of wife he wants: young – 'she shal nat passe twenty yeer', and malleable – 'warm wex'. The Merchant makes it clear that January thinks of his young wife as a commodity to be possessed.

Lines 257-364 He listens to the contradictory advice of his brothers, Placebo and Justinus, though he rejects any views that do not match his exaggerated image of marriage. Placebo, faithful to his name, does not give advice but merely agrees. Justinus echoes the Merchant himself by referring to his own experience of marriage. He also supports his views by citing authorities, which January defies: 'Straw for your Senek!'

Lines 365-483 January moves towards fantasising the pleasure that marriage to a young wife will bring him, as in lines 388-9:
> He purtreyed in his herte and in his thoght
> Hir fresshe beautee and hir age tendre.

Here Chaucer is making explicit the theme of the difference between fantasy and reality. He also emphasises January's lack of spiritual awareness as he compares the pleasures he hopes to obtain from marriage with those of Heaven.

Lines 484-496 This section describes the wedding of January and May. It is an extremely short section, suggesting that the holy sacrament of marriage was not of paramount importance to January. It seems just a quick skip through the conventions of the marriage service; even the priest seems in a hurry, as in line 494: 'And seyde his orisons, as is usage'.

Lines 497-605 The marriage feast is described with romantic imagery, suggesting wealth and culture, though the presence of Venus and Bacchus imply a certain sensual licentiousness. It is during the marriage feast that Damyan is introduced, and the reader is left in no doubt that he is going to introduce the uncertainty in the story, as in line 574: 'Lyk to the nadder in bosom sly untrewe'.

Lines 606-653 Chaucer's description of the wedding night brings in a rather sour note of reality. The close-up description of the slack skin on January's neck and his hoarse singing is an unpleasant contrast to his earlier idealisation of the married state. May's internal commentary on January's love-making is not very elegant: 'She preyseth nat his pleying worth a bene' (line 642). The wording of her image recalls to the reader January's anticipation of the joys of marriage: 'noon oother lif is worth a bene'.

Lines 654-808 Damyan and May exchange love-letters but Chaucer ensures that they are not perceived as romantically idealised figures by describing May's reading of Damyan's letter in the toilet, then her casting the fragments into the 'privee'. Damyan recovers from his love-sickness ludicrously quickly and rushes to bow to January like a 'dogge for the bowe'.

Lines 809-1006 Here the Merchant describes how January creates a beautiful walled garden for May and himself to amuse themselves in. The implicit comparison with the Garden of Eden is shocking and would remind Chaucer's audience of the terrible consequences of the Fall of Man. January keeps the only key ('clicket') to the gate ('wicket'), reinforcing the theme of property. Only he can obtain access to the garden and to May. In the middle of his good fortune, January is struck blind and May is able to take an imprint of the key in wax so that Damyan may make a copy. One spring day, Damyan precedes them into the garden and climbs a pear-tree to wait for May.

Lines 1007-1107 The Merchant digresses from his main story to describe how Pluto and Proserpina come from the Underworld to take gentle exercise in the garden. They argue about the deception of January. Pluto asserts that he will restore January's sight if May deceives him, and Proserpina says she will ensure that May has a good excuse: 'a suffisant answere'.

Lines 1108-1206 The climax of the Tale is the deception of January. May professes to long for a pear (using the excuse that pregnant women have strange longings). She climbs on January's back to reach Damyan in the tree. When they begin to make love, Pluto keeps his promise and restores January's sight. He yells when he sees his wife and servant in an embrace. But as she had promised, Proserpina gives May an excuse: she had been told that to 'strugle with a man upon a tree' would restore his sight. Chaucer gives the reader the impression that January chooses to accept her excuse rather than lose her. Though January has been given back his sight, he chooses to remain blind to the consequences of his rash choice of bride.

Lines 1207-1228 The Epilogue to the Merchant's Tale is spoken entirely by the Host. He has perhaps been influenced by the cynicism of the Tale, and claims that the Merchant has proved that women are deceitful. His short description of his unhappy marriage is his 'tale'. This conversation also takes the reader back to the framework of *The Canterbury Tales* and to the idea of the pilgrimage. Once again the reader questions the Merchant's motives for undertaking a spiritual journey.

Chaucer's pilgrims

In order of appearance:

The Knight	brave, devout and unassuming – the perfect gentleman
The Squire	in training to follow in the Knight, his father's, footsteps, a fine and fashionable young man, and madly in love
The Yeoman	the Knight's only servant, a skilled bowman and forester
The Prioress	a most ladylike head of a nunnery; she takes great pains with her appearance and manners; she loves animals. She is accompanied by another nun and three priests, the nun and one priest also telling tales
The Monk	fine and prosperous looking, well-mounted; he loves hunting
The Friar	cheerful and sociable, he is skilled at obtaining alms from those he visits, particularly the ladies
The Merchant	rather secretive; his main interest is commerce
The Clerk	thin and shabby, his passion is scholarship; he spends all he has on books
The Sergeant at Law	a judge at the assize courts; skilled at making personal profit from his office; one of the few pilgrims about whom Chaucer says very little
The Franklin	wealthy and hospitable landowner and a JP; but not a member of the aristocracy
The Five Guildsmen	although they pursue different crafts or trades, they belong to the same social guild – rather self-important townsfolk

Chaucer's pilgrims, as depicted in a nineteenth century painting

The Cook	brought along by the Guildsmen; although he is a versatile cook, Chaucer suggests his personal hygiene could be improved
The Shipman	weather-beaten master mariner and pirate
The Doctor of Physic	finely dressed and a skilled medical practitioner; he is an expert in astrology and natural magic; he loves gold
The Wife of Bath	skilled at weaving; her chief claim to fame is her five husbands
The Poor Parson	the only truly devout churchman in Chaucer's group; he avoids all the tricks unscrupulous clerics used to get rich, and spends his care and energy on his parishioners
The Ploughman	the Parson's brother and, like him, a simple, honest hard-working man
The Miller	tough, ugly and a cheat
The Manciple	responsible for organising the provisions for the lawyers in one of the Inns of Court – a plum job for a clever man
The Reeve	unsociable, but able; the estate manager of a young nobleman
The Summoner	an official of a church court; corrupt, lewd and offensive
The Pardoner	another unpleasant churchman; he earns money by selling 'pardons' from Rome, and by letting simple folk see the fake holy relics he carries
The Host	the genial landlord of 'The Tabard', who accompanies them on the pilgrimage, and organises the storytelling
Geoffrey Chaucer	he depicts himself as rather shy and unassuming.

They are later joined by another story teller, **The Canon's Yeoman**, a servant whose tale betrays his master's obsessive interest in alchemy.

Pilgrims and pilgrimages

Pilgrimages are journeys made to sacred places, usually as acts of religious devotion. They became increasingly popular during the twelfth and thirteenth centuries, at the time when the threats to Christianity from infidels and heathens, as Chaucer would have described them, reached their height. The passion to defend and reaffirm the power of the Christian church manifested itself in Crusades to the Holy Land, and an upsurge in religious fervour. Shrines were established in many European countries in places of great religious significance. In England, Canterbury Cathedral was the site of the assassination of Archbishop Becket; Walsingham in Norfolk became a holy site of pilgrimage after visions of the Virgin Mary had been seen there. The great cathedral city of Cologne was another centre of pilgrimage, as was Compostela. Further afield, many pilgrims made the long journey to Jerusalem itself, available for visits from Christian pilgrims after the Emperor Frederick II had negotiated peace with the 'infidels', and had himself crowned king of the holy city.

Pilgrims, travelling in groups for companionship and safety, would travel to shrines at home and abroad to celebrate their devotion to the church, to seek pardon for their sins, and to ask favours of the saint whose relics were preserved in that place. The traditional image of a pilgrim is of one who travels humbly and simply, dressed in plain clothes, often on foot, carrying a staff. The emblem of a pilgrim is the scallop or cockle shell, worn on cap or hood. This was particularly the symbol of St James, patron saint of military crusaders, and the journey to his shrine in Compostela, northern Spain, was, and still is, one of the great pilgrim routes across Europe. The shells may originally have been real ones, but were later moulded in lead, as were most other pilgrim badges.

By the time Chaucer decided to use a group of pilgrims as a framework for his *Canterbury Tales*, reasons for pilgrimage had become less exclusively devotional. It was certainly a profitable business for enterprising people, as well as a popular pastime. The tourist industry began to take off. The Venetians offered a regular ferry service carrying travellers to and from the Holy Land. The monks of Cluny, the greatest religious house in France, ran a string of hostels along the entire route between their monastery and Compostela. Travel guides were produced, giving information about accommodation available along the route. One for Compostela contained useful Basque vocabulary, and a description of what to see in the cathedral. Horse dealers did a healthy trade hiring out horses to pilgrims.

There was great competition for popular relics between the religious establishments, which sometimes led to rather obvious forgeries. At least two places, for instance, claimed to possess the head of John the Baptist. Pilgrims began to bring home their own souvenirs, and to house them in their local churches, like the fourteenth century traveller William Wey, who proudly deposited in his Wiltshire village church his maps, a reproduction of St Veronica's handkerchief, which he had rubbed on the pillars of 'the tempyl of Jerusalem', and a large number of stones picked up in sites around the Holy Land. Badges and emblems made of lead were sold at shrines, and eagerly purchased as souvenirs by travellers – the cockle shell for St James, the palm tree from Jericho. At Canterbury it was possible to buy an assortment of badges – an image of the head of the saint, St Thomas riding a horse, a little bell, or a small ampulla [bottle] to hold sacred water. Permission was given from Rome for the local religious houses to obtain a licence to manufacture these.

This ampulla shows Thomas Becket and his murderers

Some of Chaucer's pilgrims seem to have genuinely devout reasons for visiting Canterbury: the Knight, for instance, has come straight from his military expeditions abroad, fighting for Christendom, and his simple coat is still stained from its contact with his coat of mail. On the other hand, the Merchant does not seem to have any spiritual motives for joining the pilgrimage. He seems to be using it to advertise his expertise, and as an occasion to impress as many people as possible with his fashionable clothing and boasting. By using a pilgrimage as the frame on which to hang his stories and characterisations, Chaucer was able to point out the way in which attitudes and standards were changing and old values were being lost.

103

Geoffrey Chaucer

BIOGRAPHICAL NOTES

1340?   The actual date of his birth is uncertain, but he was near 60 when he died. His father and grandfather were both vintners – wealthy London merchants, who supplied wines to the king's court.

Chaucer was introduced to court life in his teens. By the age of 16 he was employed in the service of the wife of the king's son, Lionel, later Duke of Clarence.

1359   He fought in France in the army of Edward III. He was captured and imprisoned, but released on payment of his ransom by the duke. Chaucer was clearly valued by the king and other members of the royal family.

In the **1360s** and **1370s** he was sent on diplomatic missions to France, Genoa, Florence and Lombardy.

1360s   He married Philippa de Roet, a maid-in-waiting to Edward III's wife, Queen Philippa. Philippa Chaucer's half-sister was Katherine Swynford, third wife of John of Gaunt. The link with this powerful Duke of Lancaster was an important one; the duke was Chaucer's patron and friend, who in later life gave Chaucer a pension of £10 a year.

1368?   Chaucer wrote *The Book of the Duchess*, a poem on the death of Duchess Blanche, first wife of John of Gaunt.

1374   The position of Comptroller of Customs for the port of London was given to Chaucer, and in the same year the king granted him a pitcher of wine daily. Other lucrative administrative posts became his later.

1374-84   Chaucer wrote *The Parliament of Fowls* and his unfinished work *The House of Fame*.

1386   Like the Franklin in *The Canterbury Tales*, Chaucer was appointed 'Knight of the Shire' or Parliamentary representative for the county of Kent.

Early 1380s   He wrote *Troilus and Criseyde*.

It seems that, in spite of the royal and noble patronage he enjoyed, Chaucer was an extravagant man, and money slipped through his fingers. In 1389 he was appointed Clerk of the King's Works by Richard II, but the position lasted only two years. It may be that the poet lost his official position and favour during the political upheavals of Richard's reign. Richard later gave him a pension of £20 for life, which Chaucer frequently asked for 'in advance'. Threats of arrest for non-payment of debts were warded off by letters of protection from the crown.

1388?	Chaucer probably began to formulate his ideas for *The Canterbury Tales* at this time.
1391	He was appointed deputy forester (an administrative post) in Petherton, Somerset, and may have spent some time there.
1399	Henry IV, son of John of Gaunt, became king, and Chaucer was awarded a new pension of 40 marks (about £26), which allowed him to live his few remaining months in comfort.
1400	Chaucer died in October, and was buried in Westminster Abbey.

CHAUCER THE WRITER AND SCHOLAR

Although Geoffrey Chaucer was widely travelled and actively involved in diplomatic life and the court, he was also an extremely well-read man. His works show the influence of classical writers, as well as of more recent French and Italian works. The wide range of biblical, classical and contemporary literary references in the Merchant's Prologue and Tale bear witness to his learning, and he confesses to owning 60 books – a very large library in those days. Many of the ideas and themes in *The Canterbury Tales* have been adapted from the works of classical and contemporary sources known to Chaucer and to at least some of his audiences.

His earliest works, such as *The Book of the Duchess*, show the influence of courtly and allegorical French love poetry, in particular the *Roman de la Rose*, a dream poem about the psychology of falling in love.

The *House of Fame*, an unfinished narrative poem, shows influences from both French and Italian poetry. Chaucer admired Dante's works, as well as the writings of two other Italians, Petrarch and Boccaccio, which he came across whilst on diplomatic business in Italy. In fact, Boccaccio's *Decameron*, written forty years or so before *The Canterbury Tales*, employs the linking device (in his case a group of sophisticated men and women, entertaining one another with storytelling in a country retreat, whilst the Black Death rages in Florence) that Chaucer was to use later with far greater subtlety, variety and skill.

In both *Troilus and Criseyde*, his re-telling of the tale of love and betrayal at the time of the Trojan War, and *The Canterbury Tales*, Chaucer shows the debt he paid to classical writers, in particular Ovid and Virgil. He was well acquainted with the Bible (both the Old and New Testaments and the Apocrypha) and he knew something of the writings of theologians respected in the Middle Ages, such as St Jerome and St Augustine. He greatly admired the Roman philosopher Boethius, whose work *De Consolatione Philosophiae* (The Consolation of Philosophy) he translated from its original Latin into English. His writing shows an interest in astronomy and astrology and he wrote *A Treatise on the Astrolabe*, explaining the workings of this astronomical instrument, which he dedicated to 'little Lewis', presumably a young son who died in infancy – we hear nothing of him later.

Merchants in Chaucer's day

In the fourteenth century the merchant class was experiencing a time of increasing prosperity and expanding markets. By the time of Chaucer's death in 1400 merchants were trading all over the known world. There was very little distinction between a prosperous merchant's business and a bank, and banks were beginning to rely on promissory notes rather than the more risky transportation of bullion. This meant that a paper stating an agreed sum would be given by one branch of a bank, or merchant's business, for example in London, and exchanged for cash in another branch, possibly in another country. As there were more than 70 different currencies, a paper 'bill' of this kind, which could be exchanged for local currency, made payments marginally more straightforward.

With the increase in trading ventures came a corresponding increase in debt. Merchants frequently loaned large amounts to their clients. Although Chaucer describes his merchant as being in debt, it does not necessarily follow that he was a poor man, a trickster or even an inefficient merchant. Perhaps today we might describe him as having a cash-flow problem. He is certainly concerned with his bargains and his balance-sheet.

Money lenders in Italy, late 1300s

Chaucer's Merchant seems well-travelled; he is wearing very fashionable clothing including a hat from Flanders. He is also interested in the protection of sea trade routes. He tells a story set in Italy, specifically in Lombardy which was a city-state well known for its high number of merchant bankers and money lenders. It is entirely suitable that he should tell a tale of a knight, someone of higher status than himself, but that January should be as concerned about 'chevissaunce' as he is himself. Chaucer is thus suggesting that the Merchant has a high opinion of himself, and is justifying his own interest in goods and property.

Many aspects of the Tale, especially the character of the knight himself, seem to be influenced by mercantile imagery. Just as today, where adverts sell us a fantasy image of ourselves with a desirable object, January looks in the 'commune market place' to select a wife who suits his 'heigh fantasye'.

Many of the merchants of Chaucer's day were wealthier than some of the nobility. Perhaps Chaucer is suggesting that the Merchant has delusions of grandeur and that, by choosing to tell a tale which is partly based on courtly love and the courtly concept of 'gentilesse', he is hoping to be seen as 'gentil' himself. If so, his frequent use of the language of the market-place exposes his real character.

Courtly love

At a time when marriages were a matter of alliances and of business, love was considered an irrelevance. Brides were chosen for their dowry (the money they would bring to the marriage) or for their status. Sometimes when the man was wealthy, as in the case of January, a bride would be chosen for her looks and potential as a mother.

Courtly love was part of the chivalric code of behaviour and existed more as a literary device than a real historic practice. Conventionally, a nobleman who fell in love with a woman of equal or even higher status proved his love by performing noble deeds in her honour, or by writing poetry and songs about her beauty. Love was experienced as a kind of sickness over which the lovers had no control. The knight was not supposed to tell his lady of his love, but to suffer in silence until she took pity on him. Courtly love was not restricted to courtship leading to marriage, and so could sometimes be presented as adulterous, but in poetry it was often given a kind of quasi-religious significance with the love of a noble lady leading the knight to perform selfless deeds of heroism.

The affair between May and Damyan is a ludicrous parody of courtly love. He is not a knight and he performs no great deeds for his lady. She is not worthy of his worship. Their sordid little liaison is based on lust.

Chaucer makes the parody even more significant by his use of the old folk-tale of the pear tree. One of the sources for the pear tree story is Boccaccio's *Decameron*. In the ninth story on day seven he tells of a young wife's method of deceiving her elderly husband. She pretends that anyone up the tree 'sees' those on the ground making love. Eventually, to test this theory, the husband climbs the tree and sees his wife and her lover making love on the ground. When he struggles down from the tree, she convinces him that the pear tree has made him think he saw it. Though he accepts her word, he chops down the tree.

Chaucer places the pear tree within a magnificent garden which on one level is a reference to the Garden of Eden, and on another is an inter-textual reference to another poem, *The Roman de la Rose*. Chaucer translated some of this medieval French allegory. It is based on the courtly love tradition and is about the poet's love for his lady. In the poem she is represented as a rosebud in a beautiful garden, and unlike May, is unattainable. For Chaucer's contemporary audience, January's attempt to reproduce this garden would be an example of his hubris, and his downfall richly deserved. May and Damyan's endeavour to be courtly lovers would have been perceived as coarsely comic.

The lover is allowed into the garden

The debate on marriage

Critics have often argued that much of the middle section of *The Canterbury Tales* is concerned with marriage. The four tales of the Wife of Bath, Clerk, Merchant and Franklin are centrally concerned with marriage, though several of the other tales also concern couples who are married. These four tales are linked through imagery, theme and language. They are also related because the pilgrims talk to each other between the tales and refer to the stories and to the tellers.

The debate is begun by the Wife of Bath who, in her very long Prologue, talks of her own experience of marriage. Her five marriages have been troubled because of her view of marriage as a battle that she must win at all costs. She claims that she first married when she was 12 years old and that her first three husbands were wealthy old men. She describes how she managed them by bullying them and using sexual blackmail. The best that she can say about her fourth husband is that she paid him back for all the suffering she underwent at his hands. Her fifth marriage, to a man half her age, she considers to be happy, though he used to beat her when they were first married. Eventually, she achieves mastery over this husband as well.

In contrast, her Tale is of a fairy-tale marriage between a knight at King Arthur's court who marries an ugly old woman as the result of a rash promise. Magically she becomes beautiful when he gives her 'sovereignty'. The Wife interprets the tale to suit herself and is clearly hoping to get another young husband.

The Clerk of Oxenford responds to the Wife by telling an allegorical Tale of the improbably long-suffering Griselda, married to a Count called Walter who tests her fidelity past human endurance. He makes her promise that she will never disagree with him, or disobey him in thought, word or deed. When she agrees, he has the ladies of the court dress her suitably before she leaves her father's house. They live happily and she bears him a daughter. Then he decides that he must test her fidelity. He tells her that his people do not like his choice of bride especially now that she has had a child. He says the child must be removed. When one of Walter's soldiers takes the baby away she does not complain. Again they live happily for a time and she has a son. When the son is about two Walter again tests her by taking her child. Again she shows no sign of disobedience to his will. About ten years later he tells her the people are worried that there is no heir so he has decided to send her back to her father and take a more suitable wife. She has to beg to be allowed to wear a shift to cover her nakedness on her journey back to her father's home. When the very young bride is about to arrive, Walter sends for Griselda and asks her to make his castle ready as she knows what pleases him. She warns him that a young well-bred wife will not be as used to hardship as she is and begs him not to test his new wife. When the girl arrives with her younger brother, Walter tells Griselda that it is her own daughter and son and that he was only testing her. In spite of all her suffering Griselda keeps her word and finally achieves a happy marriage. The Clerk tells the pilgrims that his story represents the relationship between Christ and his church and that earthly women cannot hope to match Griselda's patience. In his Epilogue he makes a gently ironic reference to the Wife of Bath 'and al hir secte'.

The Clerk's Tale of the loving and submissive Griselda is followed abruptly by the Merchant's own Prologue and his own experience of marital suffering. The Tale he tells is confused in style; a mixture of ironic debate, realistic description, the well-known fabliau of the pear-tree, and a folk tale. His Tale seems, in some ways, quite close to the Wife of Bath's Prologue as the character of May appears to be similar to the young Wife described there.

Although it can be unwise to look for too much identification between the tale and the teller in *The Canterbury Tales*, it does seem that Chaucer wants us to see the Merchant as deeply moved by the Clerk's Tale. He is compelled to launch into an account of his own suffering at his wife's hands during his brief marriage. At the end of his short Prologue, he says he will not speak any more about his personal experiences – however, his tale is centrally concerned with marriage.

The tale of January begins with a long eulogy in praise of marriage. As the Merchant is himself unhappily married, this must be ironic. In fact, when read more closely, it has two major strands. One is a naively exaggerated description of the ideal state of holy matrimony for the good of the soul. The other is a darker, more selfish concept of marriage as providing great conveniences for an ageing lecher. His wife is available for sex, she cannot refuse, argue or disagree with him, she will stimulate his senses with her beauty, will nurse him when ill, and be a mother of his heir.

The debate is continued by the Franklin whose tale is closer to what is expected of a romance. His story is of a marriage between a knight and a lady who begin their relationship as courtly lovers. They agree that after marriage they will combine the ideals of courtly love with the ideals of matrimony. Like that of January and May, their marriage is threatened by a young squire who falls ill with desire for the wife. He too tells her of his love and tries to get her to agree to satisfy his desires. She makes a rash promise to fulfil his desires if he can get rid of the rocks which could impede her husband's safe return. He achieves his side of the bargain and demands that she keeps her word. She eventually manages to remain a faithful wife with the help of her husband and the generosity of the young squire.

The conclusion of the Franklin's Tale, and of the debate on marriage, seems to be that love and mutual respect must be the foundations of a successful marriage.

The myth of Pluto and Proserpina

The story of Pluto's abduction of Proserpina is one of the Roman myths about the seasons of the year. A parallel story appears in Greek mythology with Hades capturing Persephone.

Pluto was the god of the underworld, of death and darkness. Proserpina was the daughter of Ceres, goddess of harvest and agriculture. Pluto saw Proserpina gathering flowers in the valley of Enna where there was perpetual spring. He fell in love with her and carried her off to his own kingdom. Ceres was so grieved at the loss of her daughter that all the plants died and winter covered the earth.

Ceres begged Jupiter, king of the Gods, to help her to release her daughter from Pluto. Jupiter agreed, provided that Proserpina had not eaten anything during her stay in the Underworld. Unfortunately Proserpina had sucked the juice from some pomegranate seeds. A compromise was reached whereby she was allowed to rejoin her mother on the earth for six months of the year, but had to return to Pluto in his kingdom for the rest. Ceres and the earth rejoice every time that she appears, and plants begin to bloom, but when she returns to her husband, everything withers and dies.

Pluto and Proserpina represent winter and spring (as do January and May), and death and rebirth, though Chaucer's Pluto and Proserpina seem very cultured and urbane for the pagan King of the Underworld and his stolen bride. Their conversation continues the debate on the nature of the relationship between men and women. Chaucer seems to intend an ironic comment on the marriage of January and May by including another couple where the bride flees from her husband for six months of the year. The Merchant is also drawing attention to the beauty of the garden – so special that it is chosen by gods and goddesses for their pleasure.

Themes in the Merchant's Tale

1 MARRIAGE
a) To what extent do you feel that Chaucer has depicted a recognisable portrait of a certain type of man in January? Are there still men today who look for a wife who will be there only to please them?

b) Can you make any deductions about Chaucer's attitude to marriage from the Merchant's Tale?

c) Do you feel that Chaucer is sympathetic to January's way of choosing a wife?

d) How much sympathy do you feel that Chaucer has for May and Damyan?

2 GARDENS
a) How does Chaucer use the symbolism of the garden and its gate to reflect the wider themes of the Tale?

b) Why do you think that Chaucer has set the seduction scene in the garden?

c) What effect does Chaucer achieve with the introduction of Pluto and Proserpina into the garden?

3 CHAUCER'S STYLE
a) Choose two or three examples of the different styles Chaucer employs in the Merchant's Tale and show how each is used to illuminate his intentions.

b) What methods does Chaucer use to distinguish between the voices of his characters?

c) To what extent do you feel that May and Damyan are merely stereotypes?

4 TALE AND TELLER
a) To what extent would you say that in the Merchant's Tale Chaucer achieved an unusually close association between the tale and the teller?

b) What do you think is the purpose of the Host's reaction to the Merchant's Tale?

5 BLINDNESS AND SEEING
a) At the end of the tale January says that he sees 'as wel as evere I mighte'. To what extent would you say that January ever 'sees' clearly during the tale?

b) In many stories where blindness is both symbolic and real, the protagonist is often brought to clearer self-perception through actual blindness. Would you say that this is true in the Merchant's Tale, either of the Merchant or of January?

6 SEXUALITY
a) To what extent would you say that Chaucer's blunt and rather coarse descriptions of the sexual themes in the Merchant's Tale reflect his moral judgement of the characters?

b) Is there any love in the Merchant's Tale?

7 IMAGERY
a) Discuss the effects of the animal imagery in the Merchant's Tale.

b) In what ways does Chaucer use the contrast between fantasy and reality in the Merchant's Tale?

c) How effective is Chaucer's use of the repeated image of wax and impression?

8 APPEARANCE AND REALITY

a) Chaucer describes some scenes with great vividness, giving the reader a powerful visual image. Choose two or three such scenes and comment on their effectiveness in the Tale as a whole.

b) There is great disparity between the idealised descriptions of January's household and garden, and his behaviour. To what extent would you say that the gap between appearance and reality is one of Chaucer's major themes in the Merchant's Tale?

Use these questions as a basis for written work or for class discussion.

Glossary of frequently-used words

abedde	in bed	lusty	happy, pleasant
aswagen	lessen	mo	more
avaunt	boast	murye	merry
aventure	danger, chance	nexte	nearest
beningnely	graciously	nice	foolish
bet	better	plesaunce	pleasure, lust
beth	be	pyrie	pear tree
buxom	obedient	sad	serious
chees	chose	sely	foolish, simple
cleped/ycleped	called, named	shaltow	shall you
clerk	educated man	sith	since
clicket	key	sooth	truly
clippen	embrace	sterve	die
cokewold	cuckold, man whose	stoon	stone
	wife is adulterous	stryf	argument
curious	careful, elaborate	trowen	believe
devise	imagine	tweye	two
disport	pleasure	verraily	truly
eek	also	wicket	gate
eft	again	wo	sorrow
flour	flower	woot	know
franchise	generosity	wolde	would
hoor	white-haired	ywis	surely
kan	knows	ywoxen	grown
lete	leave		